Expressions From The Heart Of England 2005

Edited by

Sarah Marshall

First published in Great Britain in 2005 by
ANCHOR BOOKS
Remus House,
Coltsfoot Drive,
Peterborough, PE2 9JX
Telephone (01733) 898102

All Rights Reserved

Copyright Contributors 2004

SB ISBN 1 84418 384 X

FOREWORD

Anchor Books is a small press, established in 1992, with the aim of promoting readable poetry to as wide an audience as possible.

We hope to establish an outlet for writers of poetry who may have struggled to see their work in print.

The poems presented here have been selected from many entries, and as always editing proved to be a difficult task.

I trust this selection will delight and please the authors and all those who enjoy reading poetry.

Sarah Marshall
Editor

CONTENTS

Spiritual Alphabet	Natasha Jackson	1
Ghost Drifters	Ann G Wallace	2
For All These Things	Dylan Pugh	3
A-Click, A-Clack	Edmund Saint George Mooney	3
Lady Godiva	Christopher Higgins	4
Food	John Foley	4
Look Around You	Pippa Brooks	5
The Deceiver	Joanne Starr	6
I Don't Know	Trevor Beach	7
Evil Eye	M J Deakin	7
Funeral Élégy	Wilson James	8
At The End Of Spring	Stan Baker	10
Mother To Daughter	Ann Trahearn-Hope	11
Homeless Poem	Charlie Brown	12
Time Goes On	Evelyn M Harding	13
The Joys Of Christmas	Nicola Edis	13
The Robin	Mary S Spencer	14
Inward	Mark Guy	14
Perfect Situations	Andrew John Ayres	15
Man	Michelle Rae	16
Until Death We Do Part	Jennifer Smith	17
Wales	Hannah Newman	18
Never Enough	Simon R Jones	19
Lucky Me	Stephanie Lynn Teasdale	20
Keeping The Moon A Secret	Carole A Cleverdon	21
The Cost Of Living	Carol Biddle	22
Fish	Jo Stewart	23
The Magpie	Anna Deeley	24
The Grit Of The Brit	Walter Mottram	25
The Train	Kay Liepins	26
My Toby	Lynda Heaton	27
The Allotment	Jackie Johnson	28
No Good	Madeline Morris	29
The Sun	Kiran Kaur Rana	30
What Do They Think?	Don Woods	31
The Window Into The Soul	Anthony Crump	32

Euan	E Riggott	32
Clearance Day	Lorna M Evans	33
The Churchyard	Dorothy Mary Allchin	34
The Fens Remembered	Karen Davies	35
Second Time Round	O Karvey	36
Twin Tombstones	David Light	37
My Son	Julie Brown	38
Senses	Alan Ranger	39
Hopes And Dreams	George Reed	40
Life	David J Hall	41
A Song	Fuzz (Graham O Gallear)	42
Deliberate Bubbles?	Donna Maria Fraher	42
Ethan	Barbara Goode	43
Borrowed Spaces	Chris Webb	44
Las Vegas Lament	Adrianne Jones	45
Life In A Glass	Elizabeth Kemp	46
St Davids	Sheila Culshaw	47
To The End Be True	David Carress	48
The World Today	Sylvia Coverdale	49
Cabbage Patch	Jane England	50
The Local	Carol Jones	51
Inevitability Of Life	Rhiannon Jones	52
The Outsider	John Holyer	53
I Hope There's No Class System In Heaven	Sara Harris	54
Life's Third Chapter	E S Peaford	55
Sorry	Charlotte Bates	56
Starlight	Marty Grief	57
Friendship	Jessica Pyle	57
Life Matters	Maryanne Paston	58
Our World Today	Kristy Hodges	59
Playground	John G Turner	60
A Beautiful Thing	Nikki Clare	61
Smile	Chris Gutteridge	61
Spirit Of You	Elaine Pyle	62
She's Leaving	S C Matthews	63
Memories Of Going On Holidays	The Warrior Poet - Eamon John Healy	64

Gypsy Horse	Holly Davies	65
Pouring Out My Soul	Clare Searle	66
Norfolk Boy	John Nudds	67
Springtime	Gillian Moore	68
Days In The Park	Carrie Ann Hammond	69
Moribund	Angela Edwards	69
The Doors	Matthew Gell	70
1st Contact	Dave Stewart	71
Dream Catching	Josh Brittain	72
Judgmental Love	Colleen Keywood	73
Unwanted Love	Nash	74
My Darling Wife	Jeremy Marriott	75
Make Believe . . .	Maureen Ayling	76
August 4th 1914	S J Robinson	77
Life's Rainbow	E Winifred Garland	78
The Butcher	Mark Vanner	79
Life's Reflections	Lynda Fordham	80
Friends	E W Hockley	81
Street Strummer	Barbara Robinson	82
The Robin	Amy Barrett	82
May Result In Serious Ailment	Steve Friede	83
Regrets	D M Burnett	83
Green Spaces	Joyce Hallifield	84
A Summer Day In May	Georgette Poole	84
Will I Return?	Daniel Moore	85
Waste? - Or Resource	George Beckford	86
The Fox	Wendy Coulson	87
The Truth	Mark Anthony Allibon	87
Axe Of Seduction	Sue Umanski	88
Gangster Pretend Incorporated	Billy Shears	88
The Dark Visitor	Anne Rickard	89
Ode To Keats	Maureen Woodward	89
Jolly Jihad	Diane Burrow	90
Me Bike's Got A Puncture!	Tony Pratt	91
A Christmas Parcel	Eileen Thomas Davies	92
After Tea! James Said	Hilary Jill Robson	93
Galaxy	Stuart Feek	94
A Forgotten Part Of England	Martyn Suddaby	94

Title	Author	Page
Common Knowledge	Mea Tate	95
Dreams Of The Heart	Sheila Giles	96
Winter Rears Its Ugly Head	Paul Clarke	96
Fantasy	Emmanuel Ntezeyombi	97
Winter Glass	Bobby-Joe Parker	98
A Dream	Alice Tarran Banks	99
Mother	Elaine Hicklin	100
Youth	Kathryn E Needham	101
Shine On (A Ballad)	Hardeep Singh-Leader	102
Train Journey	Beverley Morton	103
Shame On Me	Kate Ransom	104
In The Eye Of The Beholder	Brian Ford-Powell	105
The Power Of The Word	Daniel Adams	106
After She's Gone	Teri Manning	107
My Natural High	Anya Lees	108
Kingfishers	Dan Pugh	109
Seaside	Sheila Cheesman	110
River Severn	P A Findlay	111
My Uncle's Dying	Rebecca Smith	112
Blue Sea	Garry Bedford	112
It's All Talk	Emily Watts	113
Being You	Trevor Brammah	114
The Death Of DC Oake	Lianne Kemp	115
Slowing Down	T G Bloodworth	116
Books	Connor Law	117
Judgement	Benjamin Puyenbroek	118
Weather Report	R W Meacheam	119
My Spectacles To Anywhere	Julia Pegg	120
Another Night	M Woolvin	121
Mommy, Please, Please Can I Stay?	Karen Whitehouse	122
What I Saw	H S Burn	123
If I Was An Angel	Sarah Streeter	124
Thanks	Catherine Boal	125
My Promise	Lucy Bradford	125
Each Little Soul	Dorothy M Mitchell	126
A Beautiful Love	Tracey Lynn Birchall	127
Blake Marsh	N M Beddoes	127

Title	Author	Page
Hope	J G Ryder	128
Circular	Graham Freestone	128
Monnie B'	Gary Liles	129
Day In The Life Of A Mum	Neil Warren	130
I Was A Tulip	Keith L Powell	131
Father Bus 4 Sale	Devon Stewart	131
Beyond The Rainbow	Salli Noble	132
A Musical Reflection	Enid Hewitt	133
Untitled	Debbie Alexander	134
Keepin' Up!	Lyn Sandford	135
I Believe In Aliens	Emily Jenkinson	136
Boo!	Katie Ambroziak	137
First Day At School	Mary Daulton	138
The Sea	Jane Tomlin	139
Want To Build Bridges - Not Walls	Rosie Hues	140
The Kite	Adrian Mason	141
Butterflies In The Black Forest	G Hammler	142
Love's Eye	Robin Morgan	142
A Poacher's Tale	W J Oliver	143
The Wind Turbines Of My Mind	John W Skepper	144
A Tonic From Our Father	Marina Pugh	145
On The Shelf (Again)	Norma Spillett	146
Drawn	Vivien Steels	146
Daily Reflections	Josie Pepper	147
Stranger On The Shore	John Clarke	148
Frozen	Edwin Page	148
Ancient Oak	Jan Harris	149
Late Night Break	M J Gray	149
Past Time	Luke Kayne	150
Salvation	Caroline Roe	150
Nothing But . . .	Danielle Watts	151
What's In A Marriage?	Cheryl Campbell	151
A Lincolnshire Yellow Belly	Len Woodhead	152
Heaven	Helen Drewett	153
Autumn's Strategy	Margaret Pagdin	154
Bell, Book And Candle	Jennifer Davey	155
Laughter And Tears	Judi Whitehouse	156

Being	W E Deweltz	157
Untitled	Janet Erskine	157
Babbling Brook	Ronald Claxton	158
Fade You My Love This Night	Christopher W Wolfe	158
A Summer Day Of Discoveries	Stella Bush-Payne	159
The Song Of The Fly	Edward E Gregory	160
A Friend Is . . .	Tania M Taylor	161
Nostalgia	Jacqui Beddow	162
The Ballad Of The Burnt Out Clutch	John Belcher	163
Ballad	Dorothy Buyers	164
Traffic Lives	Shirley Cawte	165
Another Realm	Henry Disney	166
When You're Not There	Sarah Sproston	167
This World	Korena Marie Baker	167
Life And Love	Sarah Clark	168
Sally Brown	Zoe French	169
Been Done Before	Peter Asher	170
One Rule	Stuart Wood	170
Love's Black Truth	Bryony Freeman	171
Malvern Hills	Ann Thompson	171
A Hill In Korea	Ron Martin	172
Mother	Ruth Fellows	173
Fairies	Emma Jane Lambert	174
A Forest Scene	Alan J Morgan	175
Friendship	Ayleen Brown	176
I Know	Ron Martin	177
Music	Muriel Webb	177
The Zombie	Adam Poole	178
Our Granny	E Marcia Higgins	179
Fear	Damian Lomas	180
Love Is A Renga	Mick Nash	181
The Devil May Care	W J R Dunn	182
Urban Demise	Wendy Brittain	183
Addict	Sheila Jane Hobson	184
Patience Required	Brenda M Hadley	185
In My Time	V Sinclair	186

The Second Lease Of Life - *Retirement*	Diana Joy Hawes	187
Arden Is Gone	David Daymond	188
An Anthem To A Chip Shop In Winter	Chris L Robbs	189
Sidney Snail	Gwen Spriggs	190
Who?	Terry J Powell	191
Collision Course	Heather Williamson	191
Tempered By The Weather	Margaret Meagher	192
Born Again?	Betty Nevell	192
Mommy Please	Carol Brierley	193
In Memory Of My Dearest Nan	Sharon Campbell Jay	194
A Fenland River	Margaret Howlett	195
Death's Rattle	Becky Keeling	196
Animal Kingdom	Callum Stewart	197
The Beautiful Garden	Adam Hedge	198
Can Doggy Poo Be Banned?	Richard Langridge	199
Out Of The Blue	Tina Brailey	200
It's Raining	Charlotte Watkins	201
Tinky's Gone	Sheila Podesta	202
All Will Be Well	Doreen Lawrence	202
The Now	Pete Harris	203
Old Photos	Ztan Zmith	203
Memories Of Our Holiday	Stan Gilbert	204
Unbeatable Sounds	B Wharmby	204
I Think Of You	John L Pierrepont	205
The Knights	Vic Calladine	206
The Haunted House	Sharon Lambley Dzus	207
Bedtime Baby	Sarah Tyrrell	208
Depression (The Accused)	Rachel Kate	209
Inspirational	James S Cameron	210
Tranquillity	Jacqueline Ann	211
Togetherness	Joan Marrion	212
The Night Sky	Emily Lunn	213
Our Baby, Our Boss! 1990-2003 Little Daisy Dolittle Devlin	Gillian Corrigan Devlin	214
Time Is Ticking	John Carter	216
My Daddy	Grace Divine	217

Being The Sofa For Doctor Who	Alex Billington	217
The Sea	J H Bennetts	218
Hope Lost	Jayne Shepherd	218
Four Letter Words!	Gerald S Bell	219
Guilt	Jacqueline Ann Johnston	219
Harry Who?	Dolly Harmer	220
Sunday Tea	Mark L Moulds	220
Over A Rainbow	Shaheen Akhtar	221
Untitled	Joanne Patchett	222
Daily Reflections On Being A Mum	Jo Willbye	223
It Seems Like Only Yesterday	Winsome Mary Payter	224
Time To Go	Graham Punter	225

SPIRITUAL ALPHABET

A lways there is the Lord for me
B eloved saviour art thine.
C aring daily for my needs
D evoted friend of mine.

E ach day I give Him thanks and praise
F or all He has gone for me.
G race and mercy abide in my life,
H is love He gives so freely.

I t's been from my youth
J esus changed my world,
K eeping me safe
L oyal to His word.

M orning arise and I give Him thanks
N ight-time I praise Him again.
O beying His word and will for my life
P ersevering until the end.

Q uiet is His presence in my midst
R adiating warmth to my heart,
S oothing are His words to my every care
T enderness never to depart.

U nited as one is the Lord and I
V enturing through my trials together.
W itnessing to all of His wondrous works,
X mas was His birth,
Y es my Lord,
Z ealous for Thee I will be.

Natasha Jackson

GHOST DRIFTERS

Whilst sleep holds the mortal form,
And dreams whisk the soul away to other worlds,
The shape shifters appear,
Smoky-grey, wispy swirls that drift in the night,
Rising up in spiralling forms,
Bending, swaying, hiding,

From dark corners,
The stalking predators peer,
Waiting to pounce,
Menacing strangers,
Inhabiting our space,
Whilst we slumber,

Acrobats that move in mid-air,
Wall to wall,
And stealthily pass through doorways,
We wake in the early hours,
Eyes half open,
To be confronted by them,

As they leap across the duvet,
Prancing to some inaudible sound,
And tiptoeing across the pillow,
In unison,
Merging and separating,
They relish our fear,

Their movements peak in a frenzy,
Our heartbeat rapidly escalates,
And then at the light of dawn,
They vanish back to obscurity,
To some distant land,
Where only shadows are welcome.

Ann G Wallace

FOR ALL THESE THINGS

For that dark void which no longer exists
In my life's centre: for the emptiness
You filled with that first smile, the gentle way
Its light filled out each corner of my heart.

For the new dawn each morning, and the rain
Which washed the leafless trees the day that we
Got married turned to trembling diamonds as
A winter sun broke through the sullen clouds.

For stillness, and the silence, when plain words
Are no more use: those times a glancing touch,
A look says so much more, and love's enough
For both of us. For all these memories

Of past, and for the present gifts: but most
Of all for futures yet to come - your smile
Upon our children's faces, our grandchildren's eyes -
These wonders make me love you most of all.

Dylan Pugh

A-CLICK, A-CLACK

A-click, a-clack, a-click, a-clack, you dragged,
That vile and monstrous curse, into my lagged,
Boarded pipes and plumbing, a terraced home:
Is this the beetle black? Why does it roam?

It sniggered, with fog-stained jaws incomplete:
It inflamed old superstitions seat:
'Shall I,' it sang, 'never cease to stop grinning?
O shall I, shall I, ever cease beginning?'

Edmund Saint George Mooney

Lady Godiva

Naked through Coventry streets, Lady Godiva rode,
in the 11th century, from a less than humble abode,
with only long hair to hide a fleshy bosomy form,
wearing just a smile, dressed the way she was born,
a wife of Leofric, Earl of Mercia, parading her skin,
staring at her flowing locks, hoping to see what's within,
young men watch her riding by, for an hour and a quarter,
some wishing that her long hair was somewhat shorter,
by the time she rides down our road, for a good view,
she may be too far away, a 100 yards distant, maybe two,
the saddle giving a bare Godiva bottom some grief,
watching her, as she canters by, in total disbelief,
Leofric would reduce taxes, if his wife did this ride,
'Peeping Tom' saw her and was punished, sight denied,
eyes hiding behind all windows and doors, of course,
all hot-blooded males, wishing they were the horse!

Christopher Higgins

Food

Food, glorious food
There's nothing quite like it,
So get in the mood.
If you've had a bad day,
Don't waste away.
A good hearty meal
And you'll feel OK.

John Foley

LOOK AROUND YOU

The sun shines in the sky,
bright and high,
It reaches into your heart,
warms the coldest
and melts the frozen.

In my sky,
the clouds fill my thoughts,
drowning the hopes, fears,
aspirations.

Raining in on the deepest emotions,
the sourest of feelings,
soaking you through to the bone,
drenched in water, rain, sadness.

Maybe, when you look up,
you will think to yourself,
that man, next to you,
does his sky shine, bright and hopeful,
or do clouds black out, cover the emotions within?

Pippa Brooks

THE DECEIVER

I thought we were forever when you led me down the aisle,
Until I discovered the secret that you'd hidden for a while.
You're not the man I know anymore, you left me for another,
You lied, deceived and cheated and truly, made me suffer.

I thought you were mine for eternity, instead you've erased the past.
Seventeen years of history, that made you what you are.
You walked away from two young sons, lost without their dad,
While you live around the corner, with her and *her* child - how sad!

So many unanswered questions, no explanations gained,
Another marriage over, more hurt, deceit and pain.
Amid the trauma and bitterness, the heartbreak and the tears,
It's sad to think this is the price for all our happy years.

You left behind three broken hearts, you'll never know the cost
I hope one day when you reflect, she's worth what you have lost.
While you hide behind denial and refuse to accept your guilt,
Our future moves on without you, our lives we have rebuilt.

They say what goes around comes around, for you I hope it's true,
That one day in the future, you'll know this heartache too.

Joanne Starr

I Don't Know

The sun rises high in the sky
A cloud passes by, I don't know why
Hundreds of horses go stampeding by
Causing havoc, I don't know why
My dog should obey I really try
He just sits there, I don't know why
Birds leave this country as winter is nigh
And return again, I don't know why
Some men are bald, others have hair standing high
What's the cause, I don't know why
Girls can be chatty some so shy
Is it us men? I don't know why
When our father calls from on high
We have to go, I don't know why
Perhaps from someone knowledgeable I'll get a reply
Maybe not, I don't know why

Trevor Beach

Evil Eye
(Jack Zangaro Part 1)

He couldn't look people square - straight dead in the eye,
It caused dogs to bark foaming, made the pram kiddies cry.
He kept his head lowered, hunched-back shouldered when walking.
He rarely engaged in face-to-face talking.
It wasn't a failing, a fear or contortion,
But for the sake of folks' sanity that he took this precaution.

M J Deakin

FUNERAL ÉLÉGY
(11 November 2002)

Recently
I've had feelings of mortality.
I always thought I'd never get caught
In an embassy bombing,
Or something.

And even in September last year
I stood not aghast nor fearful,
Nor spake I in tones most Biblical
About how the world was no longer
    a safe place to live in . . .

But now
I can see how I might end up
In a high-jacked aircraft
Or a bombed shopping centre.

So if I should die today
What will people say about me?

I hope
They won't mope about
And say I 'went before [me] time';

And if I should die tomorrow,
Please don't wallow in sorrow
    and cliché,
And say,
'He had all his life in front of him';

And for God's sake
Don't 'pay your respects':
My life's been Absolutely Fabulous.

I'm sorry to be leaving my family.
And my friends, my friends,
    forgive me
That you are there and I am gone.
I love you all, especially some,
Although I'll not name anyone:
I don't want to offend a friend
Or, say, shun a relation.

So if I should die now,
Please don't cry over spilt milk.

But try not to remember
What irked you about me.
Try to remember the good bits instead,
'Cos you can't speak ill of the dead,
    can you?

And forgive and forget
If I ever upset you
(And you're sure you didn't
    deserve it.)

But if I ever made you laugh,
Or happy,
Or bemused,
Laugh again and think of me.

Now stop acting like this is a funeral
    or something.

Wilson James

AT THE END OF SPRING

Stroll through a country lane,
Between the hedgerows green,
Breath in sweet country air,
So clear and fresh and clean.

As hawthorn's budding blossom,
Along its branches mass,
Forget-me-nots and bluebells grow
Among sparkling dewy grass.

Listen to the birds that sing,
Watch young rabbits play,
With the beauty of the pheasant,
As it struts across the way.

Marvel at the many shapes produced
By bush and tree,
The beauty of the flowers that
Attract the busy bee.

Birds flying to and fro
In their search for food,
A matter of necessity,
To feed a hungry brood.

On either side of the hedgerow
Farmers' fields are seen,
Containing young, healthy crops
On a countryside serene.

Only happiness and contentment
Are found in a country lane,
Whether the day be sunny,
Or it be pouring down with rain.

A country lane's a haven
For solitude and bliss,
Though the journey maybe short,
It's a trip no one should miss.

Stan Baker

MOTHER TO DAUGHTER

It seems like only yesterday,
That I held you in my arms,
So fragile, full of innocence and purity,
And I knew I needed you,
Just as much as you needed me.
I held you tight and nourished you,
Protected you through the years.
I played with you; I laughed with you,
Bathed your knee and dried your tears,
And the bond that lay between us
Grew stronger with each year.
Today I can't help but feel such pride,
As I see you look so beautiful,
Your new husband by your side.
I'll be here to share your happiness,
All your joys and perhaps a few tears,
And this bond that lies between us,
Will keep on growing through the years.
This bond cannot be broken,
And it will never fade away,
So I'll pray for you both to receive God's blessings,
On this your wedding day.

Ann Trahearn-Hope

HOMELESS POEM

Rough bricks against my bony body
The cold floor underneath my feet
Makes me ache all over

The smell of food all around me
Make me feel faint with hunger
And yet the sewage around my filthy feet
Makes me feel sick

The way people look at me
Makes me feel useless
These times I miss my family
All except Vince

The home I once had
Is now turning to a blur
Maybe I never had a home
Maybe it was all a dream

People arguing all around
Makes me wish I were dead
But the sound of an owl hooting in the far distance
Lets me know I'm happy to be alive

The starry night above my head
Makes my heart fill with happiness
The dustbins by my side
Make me feel dirty

To everyone I'm nothing
But rubbish cluttering up the street
To me
I don't know

One day I wish
I will not be a nothing
But a something.

Charlie Brown

TIME GOES ON

We are an island so great,
Is it destiny or fate
That we are governed by parliament and queen
This lovely isle of brown and green?

We are so good at self-producing,
Farmers in their fields, and coal mining.
The sky was lit up from the steel furnaces,
Ships down the slipways put smiles on the faces.

But most of it has gone across the sea,
For cheap labour making profit, not for you and me.
Great brains and people lost in this situation,
When will we again become the great nation?

Evelyn M Harding

THE JOYS OF CHRISTMAS

It's Christmas at this time of year
Now everyone's so full of cheer
Christmas trees, mistletoe and holly
The music on the radio's so jolly

The smell of dinner slowly cooking
And brandy for the hot fruit pudding
Tinsel, baubles and decorations do shine
It must be time for mince pies and mulled wine

Wonderful presents and paper fill the floor
Children's shrieks and happy faces, who could ask for more?
Crackers we pull and carols we sing
On Christmas Day the church bells do ring

Nicola Edis

The Robin

Winter is here
Christmas is near
Cold winds and ice brings snow
And the brave, small robin
Who comes searching for food
Comes looking and hopping
Leaving his prints in the snow
He is out in the cold
We are inside in the warm
But the robin keeps looking and hopping
And searching for food
His redbreast blends in with the white snow
If he needs to eat he must go looking and hopping
Leaving his trail in the snow.

Mary S Spencer

Inward

Illness has a smell
The stench of all's not well
A man who once stood tall and strong
Within short time is weak and wrong
This man who served his country well
Now struggles in a personal hell
A shadow of himself he lies
Inward, alone, in silence he cries
Nobody knows the depths he's fell
Within three months
Of that illness smell

Mark Guy

PERFECT SITUATIONS

Perfect situations just come running through my head
When I think about our love I think of you in bed
Love is just a simple word, the meaning I don't know
Where you gone now, I just wanna know?
Where you gone now, I just wanna know?

Perfect situations just go running through my brain
All the time that's passed us by and you still look the same
Time it never lasted and our love would never grow
Where you gone now, I just wanna know?
Where you gone now, I just wanna know?

Here, there, everywhere, jump and shout I don't care
Take time out, you know you should be proud
Here, there, everywhere, jump and shout I don't care
Perfect situations all around
Perfect situations all around

Perfect situations just go running through my mind
Picturing a Sunday morning you were looking fine
Looking out the window you said you'd never go
Where you gone now, I just wanna know?
Where you gone now, I just wanna know?

Here, there, everywhere, jump and shout I don't care
Take time out, you know you should be proud
Here, there, everywhere, jump and shout I don't care
Perfect situations all around
Perfect situations all around

Andrew John Ayres

MAN

Using guns, harpoons and nets,
Our seas will soon be bare,
All that natural beauty we love,
Will just no longer be there.

What can we do?
How can we make them see
Our whales and dolphins,
Have as much right to be?

They do to our animals,
As we do to man,
Why must we destroy
Everything that we can?

We were given the Earth,
Full of all that we need,
And now it's almost gone,
Because of man and his greed.

Michelle Rae

UNTIL DEATH WE DO PART

I am hurt but you are weak,
I am pained but yours will worsen,
I have cried another silent grief,
Until these tears can cry no more.
Watching over you,
I have sense and purpose,
Until the time you die.
Then forgotten tears may be cried again,
As I scream and ask you why.
For now you're watching over me,
For your death you cannot cry.
For my life has taken a beating,
But you know this will end in time.
Then we can truly be together,
Safe in each other's arms,
Nothing can then separate us,
Nothing can force us apart.

Jennifer Smith

WALES

From the wilderness mountains,
To the distance afar seas,
The white horses that graze the waves,
Unto the wind that moves the leaves.
As, like the Patchwork Mountains,
To the great expanse of trees,
A true piece of perfect nature,
As the clouds skim the seas.
The rocks that pierce the ocean,
That quilts the sordid ground,
Like the gorse that paints the mountainside,
Unto the heavens that shed no sound.
The mist that glides the mountains,
That blankets the rocks below,
Like the rain that gallops the open waves,
As the horizon begins to show.
From the gulls that dance the thermals,
To the heavens that colour the seas,
From the mountains that fill the skies,
Like the sun that shines through trees.
This place has peace abounding,
It breathes life into the past,
Always will it keep on going,
. . . Forever will it last.

Hannah Newman

NEVER ENOUGH

I sent a hundred roses to your door . . .
You asked if you could have a dozen more.
I offered you a priceless jewelled antique . . .
You said that you'd been given one last week.

I bought you a Ferrari 355 . . .
You said you hadn't yet learned how to drive.
I booked a champagne flight with dinner too . . .
You said that flying wasn't meant for you.

I sent a case of vintage, rare champagne . . .
You said that drink was harmful to your brain.
I had a diamond mined and set in gold . . .
You said that my design was far too bold.

I bought a painting crafted by Van Gogh . . .
You said it was a fake and made you cough.
I caught a shooting star and had it framed . . .
You said you wanted one that had been named.

I bought a yacht to offer you a thrill . . .
You said that water always made you ill.
I offered you a country house estate . . .
You said those kind of properties you hate.

I just gave up and offered you my heart
You said that's all you wanted from the start.

Simon R Jones

Lucky Me

The images just huddled round my bed,
And I was sure that I was dead.
Everything was blank and then the light,
A miracle and a wonderful sight.
I was alive although in pain,
I could see my family again.
The tubes and monitors were everywhere,
But I was alive, so I didn't care.
Needles came and nurses went away,
In and out all night and day.
So many drips and machines connected,
So many drips and tubes erected.
Friendly faces came each day
Although I couldn't remember what they said,
I didn't know really what to say
As I really thought that I was dead.
But I'm alive and things are strange
But now I must be strong,
The ghosts are all behind me now
And I'm here to sing their song.

Stephanie Lynn Teasdale

KEEPING THE MOON A SECRET

A light caresses the trees
The clouds hide the moon and stars
Where I sit there is no moon

Clouds render even Heaven opaque
Hiding the stars and keeping the moon a secret
Standing at the window wondering.

Switching off the light
Plunging myself into a familiar darkness
I walk slowly to the bedroom

No longer the moon shrouded in secret
I step into the moonbeams
Wistfully looking up into the heavens

Moonbeams that glisten on water
Like the sparkle of crystal in sunlight
No longer hiding the stars

No longer a secret moon.

Carole A Cleverdon

THE COST OF LIVING

Here am I at 28
I guess I was just born too late
My house I rent, cos though I try
I simply can't afford to buy!

What can I do to get on that ladder?
House prices are rising and I am getting madder
If I'd have been born ten years in advance
Perhaps I would have stood a chance

But now it seems written in my fate
My only chance is to emigrate
To take my husband and two children
To start a new life in New Zealand

Oh isn't that just rotten news?
I'll have to put up with magnificent views
No rat race to run, just wide-open spaces
And friendly people with smiling faces

So here's to the future whatever it brings
To fulfilling my dreams with new beginnings
And here's to New Zealand, the land of my fate
Maybe I wasn't born too late!

Carol Biddle

FISH

What you looking at?
Said the fish in the bowl
Who swam away quickly
And hid in a hole

I'm not coming out
I don't care what you say
Leave me alone
Please go away!

How would you like it?
Being stared at all day
With nothing to do
And with no one to play

So spare a thought
The next time you decide
That you'd like a bowl
With a fish inside

Going round in circles
From breakfast 'til tea
I wish it were you in here
Instead of me

Jo Stewart

THE MAGPIE

(Chorus)

Magpies are all black and white
They fly around
Looking for shiny things left on the ground
If you see money there on the road
Quickly get it before the magpie.

Verse 1

Magpies are all black and white
They fly around
Looking for food there on the ground
They fly around as fast as can be
Looking for prey for its family.

(Chorus)

Verse 2

Magpies are all black
But baby magpies are not
The difference is a lot
Baby magpies are weak and small
Big magpies are strong and tall
A baby doesn't need much to stay alive
A big magpie needs a lot to survive.

(Chorus)

Anna Deeley

THE GRIT OF THE BRIT

The GB Paralympics team
In Athens 2004
Proving beyond a doubt GB had a dream
I don't think we could ask for more

So no matter what category
Or degree of disability
They're proud to represent their country
Holding the Union Jack for the world to see

Giving 100 per cent
Finishing second in the medals
Feeling resilient and confident
Looking on in amazement to these individuals

Showing their grit
Doing only their best
In courage saying I'm true Brit
And these games have been my quest

So now it's over for the paralympic team
They can hold their heads up high
For they can say I've lived a dream
As they wipe the tears from their eyes

The spirit of the flame
Burns deep within their soul
One purpose, one aim
One unforgettable goal

Walter Mottram

THE TRAIN

The train was going somewhere
As out of the dark it came,
The girl had come from nowhere,
I remember her just the same.
The window created a picture frame,
For the girl in velvet brown;
As she sat watching the raindrops fall,
In a hat with a fringe hanging down.

Where was she going that Friday?
Who was she going to see?
Why didn't she notice me?
Was she going to meet her lover?
Her Svengali with eyes of green,
Was she already enslaved by him,
Or was she his beautiful queen?

> As the whistle blew
> The guard waved his flag,
> The train moved on once again.
> I started to move but my feet seemed to drag
> And she stared at me through the rain.

Looking through the window watching the rain,
I saw a boy in a Mackintosh, he was staring at the train.
His eyes were dark and rather intense,
He seemed to look at my hat.
Although we stopped for a moment
It registered in my mind, that he wanted to travel with me
Then we moved, he was left behind.
As long as I live I'll remember the boy at the railway track,
With eyes intense and tender, trying to call me back.

Kay Liepins

MY TOBY

You came to me at 4 months old
As a young tabby kitten, and oh so bold
You'd followed a boy, and from home strayed away
So here with me you came to stay

I put a 'found' notice in the local shop
Hoped no one would come, so you could stop
After an anxious week, and no one came
I knew then you'd be keeping your new name

I watched you grow into a fine young cat
Protecting your territory with many a spat
You'd lie in wait to launch an attack
On poor old Thomas, but he'd never fight back

You lost one of your 'lives', the worst by far
Was the night I saw you get hit by a car
The panic that filled me, I thought you were dead
When I found you lying in a neighbour's flowerbed

Luckily you survived that awful night
For a while you looked a sorrowful sight
But when back on four paws and on the mend
Into the garden you went, your territory to defend

Your antics and mischief always made me smile
Sometimes you were naughty, and I would be cross for a while
The loving cuddles we had, and the games we played
And many nights together when inside you stayed

A good many years spent together, you and me
You were the best thing in my life, that could ever be
Although you're not here now, to me you'll never die
As I still see you clearly in my mind's eye

Toby, the memories you've given me I'll always treasure
And you're here in my heart, and I've got you forever

Lynda Heaton

THE ALLOTMENT

Down in Needham Market, but I'll not tell you where
There's a place where men spend half their time with their bums
up in the air

You might ask what they're doing, have they been this way from birth?
Are they in touch with spirits or communing with Mother Earth?

Well spirits are invisible and if it's those they see
It's more likely to be the whisky, inside their flask of tea

You have to be a special kind to enjoy the scent of sewer
For not many get excited about a pile of pig manure

There are lots of home-made gadgets and known tricks of the trade
Involving plastic carriers and bottles of lemonade

There are lines of old CDs, flashing signals into space
I don't know who's receiving them but of my neighbour
there's no trace

There are water troughs and garden sheds, all with country views
The only thing that's missing is a set of public loos

So never ask a man what he's doing behind a shed
Or he might turn round to tell you, and you'll see for yourself instead

They let their onions dangle and measure each other's beans
And if no one else is looking, they'll inspect another's greens

They don't enter competitions or go in for a prize
But the length of someone's marrow, can bring tears to
another man's eyes

There are evil-smelling potions made of nettles and old weeds
Closely guarded secrets essential to their needs

They are used to douse the land, to increase fertility
Some splashed on a local girl and she gave birth to three

They say if you come at midnight at the time of Hallowe'en
With all the ghosts and ghoulies, there's a sight not often seen

For dancing round the water trough as naked as the day
Are the men with their very own ghoulies giving a ballroom display

But it's just the annual barbecue, of the allotment club
They have to hold it here because they're banned from every pub!

Jackie Johnson

NO GOOD

Sometimes things won't go my way,
No one will listen to what I say,
Don't want to believe in come what may,
I can honestly say that it isn't my day.

I do not know which way to turn,
My fire of luck just will not burn,
I only want to live and learn,
Until my better days return.

It's no good, no, I'm not dreaming,
The pressure's on, I feel like screaming,
My mind is racing, tears are streaming,
I would like to know the point and reason.

It gets rough some times, it's a fact,
I need to know how to take it, how to react,
I will brace myself for a mighty impact,
Most of the time, I will stay intact.

When it's all over and time for repair,
The end of the turmoil, end of despair,
I will have fixed myself up, mended the tear,
And will appreciate that experience was rare.

Madeline Morris

THE SUN
(A personification poem)

Blazing with fury and reddening
With rage,
The face of this stranger,
Whose presence is dominating
And whose power beyond that
Of any lawyer, doctor, politician,
Or businessman,
Bears down to look on its victims,
Who, unable to face him for long,
And unable to look him in the eye,
Begin to feel hot and uncomfortable
Under his scrutiny.
He burns with unrelentless fury
Though most of it is concealed.
Humans anger him
And one day, when they push him
Too far,
He will explode,
And kill his tormentors off
One by one, as well as
Others, who are innocent,
But have to share the damage,
As a result of others being
Careless,
And causing the destruction
Of their fellow human beings
And whose carelessness resulted
In his vandalising the entire world
And totally destroying it
Without the use of bombs
But, instead, something
Much more
Destructive!

Simply using his own full fury,
The entire existence of the world
Will be destroyed!

Then, and only then, when the world
Is torn apart,
Will his total fury be *unleashed.*

Kiran Kaur Rana

WHAT DO THEY THINK?

What do they think, I wonder
As they wander alone in the night
Through streets that are riddled with danger
Seeking refuge from the wind's icy bite

Those lost souls whose lives have no meaning
Drifting aimlessly with nowhere to go
Do their minds wander back to happier times
Maybe to loved ones that they used to know?

Fellow men cross the streets to avoid them
Eyes averted, fixedly staring ahead
They've problems enough of their own in their lives
Keeping their own families sheltered and fed

The modern world is full of indifference
For when young we are all given a choice
To abide by the rules that society lays down
Or listen to the dissenter's voice

But for those poor souls paying now for their choice
This sad life has no meaning at all
There is no turning back, no second chance
Peace will come only at the Grim Reaper's call.

Don Woods

The Window Into The Soul

Here he stares,
His eyes burning,
Like the fires of Hell,
All I can see,
Is pure evil,
Those eyes, I cannot tell,
The colour,
I can only see the evil,
I stare into his eyes,
With nothing but fear,
Not for me,
But for others,
For I do not mind dying,
I am not scared,
I feel nothing,
For fear is a weakness,
I just stare.

Anthony Crump (17)

Euan

Euan is a lovely boy.
He brings us lots of love and joy.
He grows bigger every day.
We love him more than words can say.
Soon he will have a sister or brother.
They'll get older and look out for each other.
Until then he is our pride and joy.
Our special little boy.

E Riggott

CLEARANCE DAY

Up to the attic I climbed one day
Intending to sort and throw away
The rubbish that lay upon the floor
'Twas a heartbreaking job I had in store

A doll with no hair, a battered train
A rocking horse with a tangled mane
One-eyed teddy, a cat minus a paw
Jigsaws and board games piled high by the door

Old story books, some pages torn
Cuddly toys looking sad and forlorn
A three-wheel truck, a burst football
Drawings of animals stuck on the wall

Then I paused for a moment and thought, *how can I
Destroy all my memories of days gone by
I recall little fingers that cut the doll's hair
And pulled the eye off the teddy bear*

With my eyes misted I knew for sure
These treasures would have to remain on the floor
Overcome with emotion I crept away
I'll sort out the attic another day

Lorna M Evans

THE CHURCHYARD

Behold the churchyard, sad and grim,
O'ershadowed by the cypress trees.
The breeze through the leaves,
Sings the sorrow's hymn.

Below the emerald turf they lay:
    The dead.
Those, their eyes who shall view
No more at the light of the
    Earthly day.

Branches o'er the graves bend low;
As in sympathy, fondly they entwine,
And cast their shadowed lattice
  From the pine:
Then from there upon a marble shrine,
Which glitters where the sun does glow.

Sparkles in at night, the moon's great beams
Filter, and cast out the shadows of sadness
Into glorious streams
Of these souls' immortal dreams.

Dorothy Mary Allchin

THE FENS REMEMBERED

Once sluggish streams meandered between low gravel islands
through shallow reeded lakes and swamps.
Here in this ever damp place small communities survived
and the hermit was drawn in his search for faith.
Mystic wide, forever skies reached out to the east and west
their untamed beauty back dropped by red, silver lipped clouds.

The land provided all.
A wealth of wildfowl, fish and eels were jealousy guarded.
Harvested willows and dried reeds fabricated one's crude home.
How bizarre, the sight of Fen Slodgers striding by on their stilts.
Whilst winter's freeze bore champion skaters
with their coveted prizes of money, beer or beef.

Re-modelled by man's hand.
Drainage dykes criss-cross the dark, rich fields
and modern farming methods replace the old ways.
Still, tales of Fen folklore remain, and in quiet spaces
along the empty roads and soothing waterways.
History echoes beneath the open, untamed artist's skies.

Karen Davies

SECOND TIME ROUND

How do I look? Do I look alright?
Does my hair look a mess, does my face look a sight?

If only I could ask my son but he's such a gormless dipstick
Perhaps I need a quick stiff drink but it might upset my lipstick

I wish I could just run away but I'm really rather keen
Not only is he suave and fun but also fit and lean

Oh no! There goes the doorbell, I can't believe he's early
My legs look fat, my dress is wrong, I hate that Liz Hurley

We danced and drank and ate a bit, I had such a lovely time
He held me close, I touched his bum, it must have been the wine

I didn't ask him in though, somehow it didn't seem right
I need to get new underwear before he stays the night

I've taken off my make-up and everything is spinning
My head, the door, the bathroom floor but nothing stops me grinning

I'm hoping that he'll call again, if not then that's alright
It wasn't a trial and I made him smile so I think that he just might

O Karvey

TWIN TOMBSTONES

Projected high were we,
Our flag of peaceful co-existence there unfurled.
Power erected here, midst all our peers,
Twin Towers, crowning seething world.
For envious would-be rivals too inviting.
Each slaughtered soul has joined the tons of ash, bent steel and dirt
When downed by flaming arrow.
Pause for grief.

We'll flaunt the flag on top a second time,
To reach unprecedented heights.
This magic structure rises mightier yet, and loftier yet,
No fear of wind nor quake nor fire.
A monument to enterprise,
Our shining space is shared with Liberty,
Whose heavy hand points fire at eastern lands.

As grief, displaced by surging energy, tries to own the sky once more,
Devious minds still watch
From hidden undiscovered caves,
Overseen by cruel smile.
Without a sign, the plans are laid.
Terror's hopeless actions will not wane.
Build it brazen! Fools' conceit!
Then we can knock it down again.

David Light

My Son

I've loved you forever
since that bright sunny morn
when I first held you
you were my first born.

My joy was complete
as I cuddled you tight.
My life at that moment
was, oh so right.

I heard of the pitfalls
of having a child,
and I didn't expect
you would be meek and mild.

I helped you grow up
into a wonderful boy.
The days we spent together
were full of joy.

Now you are a man
my love for you is still there,
but now you show me
all *your* love and care.

Julie Brown

SENSES

Music is my heartbeat
Truth is my blood
Openness is my sight
Trust is my hearing
Respect is my taste
Integrity is my touch
Conviction is my smell

Guided by these I seek thee out
Friendship, love and companionship
Hope but no expectation
Uniqueness in all its beauty
A person with endless scope

Giving and receiving of life's tales
Stepping ever closer to each other
Synchronicity without time
A joining of souls and merging of spirits
Filling the space yet growing the capacity

Enriching the contents but not altering the meaning
Allowing the vulnerability willing to trust
Revealing the history but not carrying the scars
Carrying no malice, guilt, anger or pain
Daring to be truthful, sincere and unashamed

Each encounter undertaken a reason to understand
A message or guided reflection and something to retain
A soulmate, lover or friendship or even a simple connection
Long term or short lived would be wrong to determine intention
For receiving is giving and to give is a gift

Alan Ranger

HOPES AND DREAMS

Thank you for trusting me with your cares and woes
No doubt you are trying to keep me on my toes,
Jesus did say, 'It wouldn't be an easy life
Because Satan likes to cause lots of trouble and strife.'
Family life is his favourite target or so it seems
Where he loves to shatter all our hopes and dreams,
Of two or more who hope to live happily together forever
Satan likes to cause stress and division so that we can never,
Be truly carefree and have a life full of joy and fun
Because if we were it would mean there'd be no work to be done.
Satan knows how easily it can be to cause trouble between
                                        the people of Earth.
That's why he tries to cause mistrust and division for all he is worth,
Our lives need to be centred on Jesus Christ, God's beloved Son
For only through Jesus can this Earthly battle be won.
Because only through Him can we get an answer to prayer
For He knows about our problems and how to Him we can share,
All our doubts and our insecurities too
Because He knows everything about us, me and you.
So don't let your problems get you worried and down
Take them to Jesus and let Him give you a smile, not a frown,
Our trust and faith need to be on our God above
And through prayer He will protect and cover us with His love.
So put Satan behind you and give him not a thought
But fix your eyes on Jesus like you know you ought.

George Reed

LIFE

Life, what is life?
Life is living
Alive, breathing
Life is fun
Life is hell at times
Life begins, life ends
Life for some is short
Life for some is long
One ages in life
One does many things in life
One enjoys, one works
One goes on holidays
One travels, some go afar, some not so far
One sleeps in life
But still alive when one is sleeping
One does shopping
One does eat
One in life eats a vast amount of food
In life one can be killed
In life one dies
Then one no longer has life
One is not alive
Life is no longer life as we know it
Life has gone from one
Life no more
Spirit rises to Heaven
Spirit life begins

David J Hall

A Song

A man stuck in the doldrums, living in a plastic Mac,
The rain it falls down in streams, the concrete cold against my back,

I've walked down the streets of Whitehall, seen the fancy
Rolls and Jags,
Seen the millionaires in their pinstripe suits,
While I live in my plastic Mac.

The old lady walks with a plastic bag, at the doss house
they form a queue,
They stand in lines, side by side, for a bowl of warmed up stew.

Down beneath the arches a guitar strums a tune,
A fire crackles from a steel drum, and flickers light against the moon,
Man we're in the doldrums, is there no turning back,
The millionaires are in their pinstripe suits,
And I'm in my plastic Mac . . .

Fuzz (Graham O Gallear)

Deliberate Bubbles?

I life the wand towards my mouth
Hold my breath in and down
Letting my chest drink it in
I sit still until
        I start the flow
You say, 'No! Do it slower!'
I'd always blow too hard and
They'd backfire
        and sting my skin;
The one or two that I produced
You, made too many bubbles.

Donna Maria Fraher

ETHAN

The post had been erratic, hadn't brought me much,
Postman he kept going by, letters in his clutch.
However on this Monday, he opened wide my eyes,
Going to my letter box found to my surprise,
Large envelope was pushed through, was addressed to me,
My eldest son's handwriting, meant grandfather *new* he'd be.
We'd both shared excitement waiting for babe to come,
This made me *great grandmother* to Ethan his *new* grandson.
Lad nine pound 3 ounces, born two days ago,
Roger took photo two hours old, he proudly let me know.
Fed into computer with modern machines you can,
He was there in front of me looking at Great Nan.
A bonnie little laddie, just as his dad had been,
Skin not at all wrinkled, smooth as any queen.
His family would love him, place be so secure,
In bliss we would enfold him, now and ever more.
You love your own grandchildren, all grandparents should,
But when it's your first great one, you feel extra good.
A new limb of the family makes every bitter pill,
Swallowed while they're growing up, worth struggle up the hill.

Barbara Goode

BORROWED SPACES

How long are we here
in these borrowed spaces?
Not long enough
to be selfish
or greedy.
We give our time
to one another.
We hope
to be here tomorrow.
Who knows?
The moments we share,
precious,
priceless,
never fade.
Recorded
in the borrowed spaces
of our hearts and minds;
they stay with us.
We learn to cherish
each passing day.

Chris Webb

LAS VEGAS LAMENT

Surreal surroundings . . . surreal thoughts.
Had he just imagined the slot machine
Called out 'feed me, feed me'?
Hunched over the machine he reflects.
How had hundreds of dollars vanished so quickly?
Like a magician the machine had moved his cash
So deftly.

If he had kept his winnings when they reached
Five hundred dollars, he'd be laughing.
But like a fool he had fed the greedy chrome mouth
Putting in coins as if there were no tomorrow.

Till every last dollar had gone.

The machine was now briefly sated
He on the other hand fuelled with a few pills
And golden boy Jack Daniels.
Had not eaten all day.
And now could not afford it.

Oh well, he thought, *another day, another dollar.*
What the hell.
Life's a gamble isn't it?

Adrianne Jones

Life In A Glass

Your life is there within the glass
You say this drink will be your last
It's got a hold that's hard to break
The tears it brings, the life you forsake

You wrap your hands around the glass
You should have guessed that life would pass,
It builds you up and makes you feel good
Then destroys your world because it could

The more you drink the better you feel
This life you live is not for real,
You like to think you're in control
But like a fish, you're in a shoal

There's only one way this path you ride
The pain and tears you try to hide,
The demon drink and all it will do
You deserve better, you do, you do

Walk away while there's some in your glass
Get your life back, forget the past,
Let go of the trip before it's too late
Don't let your life be down to fate.

The lives it destroys as it gets a hold
It gathers pace, brings more to the fold,
What starts as fun soon it's too late
It's got what it wanted, and closed the gate,

Once behind you're in its grasp
The fight is on and long will it last
It's a fight you can win if you'll only be strong,
This trap you are in, you know is wrong,

So let this drink be your last
Don't let your life be set and cast
Move away from the demon drink
And you'll move quickly from the brink.

Elizabeth Kemp

ST DAVIDS

Walking hand in hand through the breeze blown grass,
round the gate, to see the chipped Virgin's face.
Votive offerings. A baby shoe the last.
Sad, boastful blue hydrangeas commonplace.
Saint Non's sacred well, full of coins, is passed
to enter the chapel. Focus on space,
the altar. Ancient pattered stones defy
intellect. Candles flame, die, sanctify.

Minutes taken each year here on my own,
reflective and sad. Run to my lover.
See cliffs purple, grey, squarely overgrown,
fighting the crashing, smashing sea. Discover
lace-edged waves and rocks below. Brown hair blown
round and round. The bright sky helps recover
quiescence. Gulls scream past the cracked,
crazy scars. Harsh winds cleanse, bring laughter back.

Sheila Culshaw

TO THE END BE TRUE

The light on the water, reflected his face,
Strong and proud, with eloquent grace.
His battle armoured plate,
Couldn't conceal his fate.

Off to war he went,
Looking for victory, heaven-sent.
A crusade, worthy of all,
Man and horse standing tall.

For king and country he fought,
A mighty lesson he'd been taught.
Stay honest and true,
And Heaven will have a place for you.

Battle lines are drawn,
But none stood forlorn.
Death when it came
Would valiant heroes tame.

An opportunity valiantly lost,
And in life, what cost?
Another warrior had been tested,
As now in angels' arms he rested.

David Carress

THE WORLD TODAY

The world today seems very bad
Wars and killings - oh so sad!
Who's to blame, why is it this way?
Don't blame the world, it's man and his say.

The world that we live in is a rotten place
Full of destruction, killings and hate
Men, women and children are no longer secure
From muggings and murder and horribly more.

Switch on TV and what do you get
More wars and massacres - it is endless!
Why can't we all live in harmony
Where everyone is happy and trustworthy?

The world today could be so good
With no more wars, slaughter or blood
If only man more pleasant would be
Listen to troubles, not fight, just see.

How happy all countries united together
Allies and friends no matter whatever
So please don't blame the world today
It is just folk and their damn way!

Sylvia Coverdale

Cabbage Patch

She bends over the cabbage field,
The morning fog around.
Her frizzed black curls hang with dew
She wields her surgeon's knife,
Cutting each orb of cabbage from its thickest stem.

A modern 'Tess' she works her row,
Black sweat upon her back; her orange trousers
Proof against the wanton tractor which
Relentlessly collects box upon box
Hour by hour. These will feed the citizens of the town.

They know nothing of her toil,
The whims of sun and rain.
They drive into town in ordered line,
Read computers row by row,
Sweating under neon lights in central heating.

At five o'clock they struggle home,
Pushing through traffic as in the morn.
Exhausted, they shower, eat and watch telly.
'Tess', rested from the mid-day heat,
Placidly cuts another row of cabbage in the evening air.

Jane England

THE LOCAL

Cigarette and cigar fog
Rise above the throng
Of 'punters' jostling
For bar space
A singer struggles to be heard
Above the shouting and camaraderie
Saturday night at the local
Weird and normal people mix
Bartenders run to and fro
Keeping demanding customers happy
As the drink flows
So does the conversation
Putting to rights
The dodgy world outside
The pub is a haven
Relax and forget your troubles
Sit beside the bar
Absorb the colourful characters
Observe the behaviour
The clothes, the hairstyles, the effort
Or not people make to come here
And when 'Time' is called
Go home and look forward
To more of the same.

Carol Jones

INEVITABILITY OF LIFE

To curtail all the bad and retain all the good
The feelings of guilt, regret and rejection
For the memories of blossom in the spring
But there is no power

Heavy weight upon shoulders and lead in the heart
Tired footsteps with mind full of weariness
Wanting to thwart contemplations before they emerge
To numb a troubled mind if but for a while

To hear the wind whisper through latticed branches
To count the blossoms as they waft on a whisper
To breathe in the sharp smell of dawn
To feel the cordial warm embrace of dusk

Acknowledgement of heavy heart when sorrowful
Yet distinguish the unconditional love
Accept the unwelcome circumstance

Understand those who walk under the evening stars
Are powerless to change what has and will come to pass
But have the capacity to enjoy and appreciate each moment

Gazing into the eyes of a loved one
Achieving a dream

Life

Rhiannon Jones

THE OUTSIDER

Stranger in town how do you survive?
Nobody knows you, who cares you're alive?
But you shine like a diamond, aloof and aware.
You are the outsider, that's why you're there.

It won't be long, no there's the first.
Do you need refreshment? Do you have thirst?
Or just conversation, a quiet little word
What do you know? What have you heard?

Well I'll tell you Sir, what you want to know.
Of Heaven above and of all Hell below.
What's that? Gone weak at the knees?
Stay for a while, let me tell you stories.

Of stress and some pain and lost love regained.
Of journeys and travels and monsters been slain.
Of a journey through time that was taken alone.
And a heart that has loved but been turned into stone.

Let me regale you with tales that need to be aired.
Of times that were happy and rage that was shared.
Of love that was true but smote into dust.
Of battles that were lost, and lots of mistrust.

So where do you go, my long lost new friend?
Won't you share in my pain? Be there at the end?
You have to leave? Well I understand.
You cannot stay here lest you be damned.

Leave now or stay if you must.
Listen to your instincts, go with your trust.
The stranger may drown you, drag you deep in despair
Look! Where he was standing, there is no one there!

John Holyer

I Hope There's No Class System In Heaven

I hope there's no class system in Heaven,
Because wouldn't it just seem like Hell,
To be no one of worth, down here on Earth,
And be nobody up there as well?

Wouldn't it be just awful,
If the first bloomin' person you met,
Was a snooty duchess, or a haughty princess,
Saying, 'You there, light my cigarette'?

I hope that up There we're all equal,
And others not more so than some,
That nobody cares, if you've got big ears,
No legs, or a great big fat bum.

I hope that the food There's not fattening,
You can eat from nightfall 'til noon,
Chips, chocolate and cake, and not end up the shape,
Of a fully inflated balloon.

I do hope that colour won't matter,
Not be used as a measuring gauge,
In fact we should be, perhaps, colour-free,
Or all painted a nice greeny sage.

I hope we'll all get the same pay There,
No matter what job we do,
Including, all those who kick a ball,
And those who clean out the loo.

I hope when I first get to see Him,
He is wearing a red baseball cap,
That He's kind and benign, with a nice glass of wine,
And a big ginger cat on His lap.

Sara Harris

LIFE'S THIRD CHAPTER

They can be seen nearly every day,
Small groups of men and women
Bunched together with little to say,
Heads shaking like puppets on a string.
Hands resting on sticks of age and time,
Fighting for memory, and the bell to ring.
Have they given up, turned aside from pride?
Or is it conscience of mind?
Where is their rage against age;
Is it so hard to find?
Or is the third chapter of life
So difficult to bear,
When an ambitious pain stabs like a knife,
At any time; anywhere?
Yet they can dream
Of the second chapter with ease,
But what happened yesterday
Was lived and now forgot,
Like burnished leaves strewn across a garden plot.
The years have gone so quickly,
Worn out like an old-fashioned song;
A little sob and a weary cry
To the memories of those they belong.
Laying still in a hospital bed,
Her aching eyes shut tight,
A soft voice of prayer is read,
The curtains shut because of the light.
Across her lips, the hint of a smile,
Was it for her Maker or us by her side?
Or was it her dignity, her style or great pride?

E S Peaford

Sorry

Jealousy ripping my heart in two
Though I have no power over you
Watching you flirt with another girl
Head and heart argue, all in a whirl.

I knew it weren't gonna happen with us
Right from the start but you must
Have known how I felt about you
I stared too much for you not to.

All through my bad adolescent phase
I cursed myself for having such a craze
Over a guy who didn't like me back
No one else would do, 'twas you or whack!

Now you're not talking to me
Cos of me being stupid and silly
Jealousy got the better, you see
Please realise, that's not the real me.

Not being able to flirt and chat, I hate
But I also have lost a brill and lovely mate
You flirted back, admit it's true
But in my stupidity, I lost you too.

I want things to go back to how they were
A laugh, a flirt, a touch, giggle with me and her
I know you're not very forgiving to someone who's done you wrong
But I'm praying you'll realise how sorry I am through this song.

Charlotte Bates (17)

STARLIGHT

Storms brewing within a heart of fire,
Void born lights riding across the night sky
Showing portents of our lives' desire,
Revealing destinies to us, from high,
And fate always reveals that we must die.
A span of time measured in hearts beating,
Too short not to fill it and then to cry
Over that beating heart's time been wasting.
Hearts, lives and the stars were designed to sing,
To be glorious, the night sky to fill.
Slivers of silver ice never melting
Holding our fates in their eternal chill;
Although our lives are our own to complete
To guide our destinies the stars compete.

Marty Grief

FRIENDSHIP

Friendship is like a circle
That grows wider every day
Friendship is a feeling
That's inside of you to stay

Friendship is a part of you
You're fond of it indeed
When my friends are helping me
I know I can succeed

Friendship is a happy thought
It lasts for eternity
I am friends with everyone
And everyone's friends with me.

Jessica Pyle

LIFE MATTERS

Murmurs in the distance, voices unknown
people in a crowd, no faces are shown,
to know someone is to see their heart
different cultures worlds apart.
Trying to find a purpose, a place in the world
searching for reasons, a place to go
searching for that someone to give life meaning.
Alone in the abyss cold and weak
still searching for meaning but the future looks bleak,
head around the corner you'll find what you seek
growing stronger every day, no longer weak.
Fighting for survival one day at a time
knowing where to turn in a time of need
knowing when to help, to do a good deed.
Knowing when to do the right thing is not always easy
but to do the right thing brings its own reward.
To help another,
to be strong and survive,
to find your place in the world,
to mean something to someone,
to have a face in a crowd and to be heard when you speak,
qualities we should all bare but we show our strengths all too rare.
All I can say on the matter in hand is . . .
Love who you are and you shall be loved,
fight for a cause and not just because,
live for the now and not for the then
hopefully everything shall have a peaceful end.

Maryanne Paston

OUR WORLD TODAY

Gone are the days when news used to bring
Moments of light to our life
Stories of courage, celebration and joy
Cast aside to make way for the strife

Turn on the television, pick up a paper
See human beings in their plight
Children and families torn apart in an instant
By beliefs that have lead us to fight

Whether Iraq or Beslam, New York or Madrid
Only the innocent pay
It feels like we're all in a lottery . . .
Which country will it be today?

We can't even turn to our leaders
To right the wrongs we see
It's they that have bred and fed this horror
By ignoring our own history

My heart goes out to those in the world
Who don't know what to do
To pull their shattered lives together
How would it feel if it were you?

The only thing that is certain
As I tuck my son in bed
Is I'll feel grateful for what I have
And not bow to a world filled with dread.

Kristy Hodges

PLAYGROUND

We did not understand
You and I just born,
To hold hands with the still,
We could only run,
So we ran,

Over the green grass damp,
Our tiny feet pelted marble scripture,
Barking profanity as we rushed,
Vandalising the moment,

To the great ash we would clamber,
To conquer its height,
To crow and confound if only for a short while,
But we failed to calculate,
Infirmity and conception,
As with pulsation at pace,

The pulverised bough in your palm,

You plummeted,

To ground, a moment of concern,
The next with laughter,
Comfortable in the comedy,
Like everything else.

Your mum all in black clipped your ear when we got back,
Mine told me I had no respect for the dead,
And the gone,
As we stood with those who were frozen over the opening
Of soil and sod,
Not understanding

Beneath our feet lay the ghosts
Their remains a reminder,
Of time and tide,
Their eyes not green by decay but with jealousy.

John G Turner

A Beautiful Thing

Life is a beautiful thing.
To sit quietly; listen to the birds sing.
To enjoy the moment; to enjoy the views;
To gain energies and replenish.
For life is to be learnt; enjoyed.
Everything in the day is new.
For everything we feel and see.
Under peace, we find integrity.
Abundantly and unconditional.
Love is love always; carried internally.
To appreciate what we see and perceive.
To appreciate this beautiful world is what we perceive.
What we perceive is not always what we see.
A beautiful thing is to resonate and accept to be.

Nikki Clare

Smile

When I see you I smile
It's as if the clouds have parted.
I feel the world's a better place
Whenever I see your face.

Quiet, contained,
But brimming full of life,
You make me feel my life's begun,
That from now on it's fun.

When you smile at me
I can't believe my luck.
My heart begins to sing
And my soul takes wing.

Chris Gutteridge

SPIRIT OF YOU

I felt your spirit
Gently flutter through my empty soul
It lifted my heart
And filled a dark hole
Momentarily I felt whole
And remembered our love
As it was when you were here
I recalled it so clear.

A pause in time
A flashback to yesteryear
To days of warmth and feeling
Of heartfelt contentment
And well-being.

Your spirit came to comfort
And deliver a message
Telling me that through the years
You've never left me
And you'll always be near.

I felt your spirit
Gently flutter through
But what I'd give
To still have you.

Elaine Pyle

SHE'S LEAVING

As your new life's journey is taking its course
You'll do lots of things and become a new force
I hope things go well for you as you travel on
For you are so lucky you can become someone

Life is a battle in some of our eyes
Though I am so grateful for you have told no lies
You'll meet all kinds of people and I hope you will see
That somebody special that's what I want to be

Don't think of the present, don't think of the past
Think of tomorrow as if it wouldn't last
Live life to the full while you have the chance
God knows your life's been no song and dance

Be happy whatever and try just to see
The kind, loving person I know you to be
Go see all the things you have in your mind
You are a good person so deserve a good time

Well now that I've said this you can just relax
Now you can get rid of those heavy sacks
The time has come and you must be strong
So go now my darling to where you can belong

S C Matthews

MEMORIES OF GOING ON HOLIDAYS

We're going on our holidays to see the sandy shore,
Our yearly treat, never fails to make our spirits sore.
We're going down to see the sea, where the waves do break,
We're going for a picnic, and our dog we're going to take.
Playing games on the sandy shore and fishing with a net,
Crabs and shell in rock pools, I'm going to get them yet.

We're building castles in the sand in happy carefree days,
Flying kites in the sky and in the sun we laze.
I only wish our holidays lasted for evermore,
On those warm, hot summer days.

Collecting shells and fancy stones,
Seaweed black and red,
It only seems like yesterday,
But now I'm ill in my bed.

Going on our holidays with our mum and dad,
Now it all seems so far away
But going makes me glad.

It only seems like yesterday. I promised to be true,
Tomorrow is my birthday and I'll be ninety-two . . .

The Warrior Poet - Eamon John Healy

GYPSY HORSE

His hooves are spread like soup plates
His legs thick like tree trunks
His ears swivelling like satellites
His eyes as deep as lagoons

His walk fast like the wind
His trot powerful like a thunderstorm
His canter rough like the sea
He jumps as if he has wings

His sides are solid and wide
His back is tall and strong
His legs are muscular and long
His tail lengthy and matted

In the field he was left to die
Watching cars and lorries storm by
In the winter he had to lie on ice
His coat was wriggling with lice

He certainly is a monstrous horse
But though his coat is rough and coarse
He deserves a better life
With a loving carer and free from strife.

Holly Davies (12)

POURING OUT MY SOUL

Just sitting here wondering who I am! I'm empty inside, nowhere to go, nowhere to hide. All alone where no one can see me. Wondering where I went wrong in my life. Wishing I was somewhere else, anywhere but here. The pain trapped inside my body, my soul, is slowly turning black. Wondering whether I was a mistake, just an accident! Looking in the mirror seeing no one, just an empty person. That's all I am, just a person, same as everyone else. I'm all alone wishing I could turn back the clocks, change the past so that it is better for when the present returns. Just sitting here writing this, pen to paper. Doing nothing special, just pouring out what's inside. Just wondering about the pain in the world, my pain. We all have to die sooner or later, sometimes I wish it could be sooner rather than later. Waiting for death, that's all, life is waiting! We enter this world alone and that's how we leave it. We haven't gained or lost since when we were born, we had nothing to lose but life itself! Take life one step at a time and make the most of it because tomorrow might be more lonely than today. Where am I going? What am I doing? There's not one person on this Earth that can tell me who or what I'm going to be. They can't tell me what to do or say or think, all they can do is stand back and watch me live my life. Although I'm waiting for the perfect life, it will never come, no one ever really has a perfect life, they may pretend but they don't. Nothing really has any importance or does it? Lots of people say money can't buy you happiness but what if it can? Who's to say it can't, people with no money to buy food aren't happy. But if you can buy everything you want, wouldn't you be happy? I know I would!

Clare Searle (13)

NORFOLK BOY

I will believe in miracles when you turn your love to me,
To know that I have found true love,
For all the world to see,
That when you look into my eyes
With passion closing in,
My love for you is evermore,
With you it did begin.

It's not till now that I have known what true love really means
And all the ones that have gone before,
Are now just old has-beens,
You can't believe it's happening,
When it's not been there before,
It's like being in a dream world,
With a key to every door.

To float on every cloud up high, great happiness at last,
Nothing will displease you,
You let it all go past,
Now that I've expressed myself,
Told you how I feel, showed you my undying love,
Which only you can heal,
I am your loving Norfolk boy,
With accent loud and clear,
We might be just old country boys,
But none are more sincere.

John Nudds

SPRINGTIME

Springtime is a time of warmth and sunshine,
Dull old times are gone for now,
Making way for the young and new.

Bulbs bloom in the garden,
Trees blossom into bud,
Bees buzz around the flowers,
Butterflies float around
Going on the air.

Baby lambs jump and frolic full of joy,
All the fluffy yellow chicks as well,
All is new and full of life.

Children dance around the maypole
Laughing and smiling as they dance,
Also they are wearing dresses
With frills and flowers all around.

Nights getting lighter, making the days longer
Sultry nights with warm air,
Making the evenings pleasant to go walking in.

Easter time is a relevant holiday,
For joy and sorrow,
Children are waiting for Easter Sunday,
When they receive their Easter eggs.

Springtime is for weddings,
All in their best attire,
Flowers, garlands smelling sweet.
Joy, tears, laughter, ring through the air.

Gillian Moore

DAYS IN THE PARK

Do you remember when we were small
down on the park, kicking a ball.
Chasing each other around the trees
falling over and scraping our knees.
Playing games of hide-and-seek
we'd count to ten but take a peek.
Climbing up to the top of the slide
down headfirst, oh! What a ride.
Losing track of time and late for tea
still on the swings, you, Johnny and me,
backwards and forwards swinging higher and higher
we'd watch the sun set beyond the church spire
and then we'd leave when darkness descended,
adventures were over, the day had ended.
Yes, I remember those days long ago
etched on my memory, I treasure them so.

Carrie Ann Hammond

MORIBUND

They say life is sweet, but not for me,
every day is an unending struggle.
How much longer have I to endure this?
Pain, weakness, wretched old age is all around me
and I can smell death approaching.
But not quickly enough, it drags itself
slowly towards me, and I fear its coming,
but welcome it too, if only it would
hasten and claim me.

Angela Edwards

THE DOORS

As I stride upon the light of day
I close the doors
Of dark pathways.
Shut out the echoes from the past,
The brutal fist,
The cursing mask.

Then darkness falls,
With impenetrable veil.
Locks unbolt,
The memories impale.
I reach for the light lying at my side,
But the sandman
Hasn't passed her by.

I grab my vest from off the floor,
Creep across the carpet to the door.
I turn to check that she's still sleeping,
Her breath confirms and I'm alone through this weakening.

The kettle is on,
My mind pounds
Head demons do their rounds.
Up and down,
Left to right,
Screeching through this hopeless night.

If they left two pints of milk at each door
I'd still have the million
From the night before.

My past has no purpose.
It messed me up,
It's useless,
It's worthless.
So let me sleep.
Oh Sandman come.
I don't wish to see the rising sun.
Don't want to feel my soul in struggle,
My sunken eyes
Imploding this bubble.

Matthew Gell

1st Contact

Worse than the sense of imminent doom,
Worse than a deadline and its subtle loom,
Worse than the beasties that make you cringe,
Worse than the diet that follows a binge.

Worse than a crunch as you are dumped on your butt,
Worse than a curry that won't agree with your gut,
Worse than those soaps as bad as 'EastEnders',
Worse than those cock-ups with the lids to those blenders,

Is the gut-wrenching fear as you start on your way,
With a tiny, small sentence all planned out to say,
And the stopping, the turning, and bolting in shame,
Having totally bottled it, not even catching her name.

Dave Stewart

Dream Catching

Swirling mists, snowy fog, faces stare at me,
Telling fortunes of the day, blind, these things I cannot see.
Voices shout, some whisper too, telling tales fair,
Visions of streets and cobbled ways, crinoline dresses flair.
A greying smile, thin lank hair, you mouth words I understand,
Flashing globes fill my head, reaching out I touch your hand.
Blinking eyes, I clear my mind, trying not to shake my head,
Grasping hard, I hear hidden thoughts: Conversations with the dead.
Marching orders; dull thud fire, echoes of the night,
Stinging, running, bloodshot eyes, I wish that I could fight.
Twilight beeches; scattered men; the slain and injured cry,
A flash of light, my knuckles white, pain makes me want to die.
Twitching; writhing, the sheets I pull, wrestling with my dreams,
Clandestine shapes mock my fate; silver tunnels make me scream.
Grasping tight, my comfort neigh, dripping sweat, I clutch and claw,
For some sweet memory, tranquil days, as pastels pictures draw,
Stone steps appear, leading up, glisten in the rain,
I hear a shout, thundering hooves, see urchins by a drain.
Silhouettes dance around a tree, Maypole garlands bright,
Full moon candles flicker strong; chanting their god's might.
Startled, waking, listening out; the visions fade away,
I'll try again to catch my dream; next time it may just stay.

Josh Brittain

JUDGMENTAL LOVE

After she died, I was shocked to discover,
that Mother had not, absolute love.
My sister's portrayal, so different of that of myself and my brother,
was judgmental, love not enough.

No one is perfect, not even a mother,
although as a child I believed her to be.
Time showed her to be quirky, extraordinary compared to the others,
but she was always 'Mother' to me.

So independent, and never a burden,
insisting on doing 'her own thing'.
Adept at the crafts, we never brought 'woollies',
and her pastry was fit for a king.

When in her nineties, she saw she was waning,
yet, still very private and proud.
She prayed to go quickly without fuss and palaver,
but shame; came the hospital before the shroud.

And so life goes on in its spiralling quest,
our offspring have offspring themselves.
How will they judge us? Please God not too harshly,
will I, like Mother, fail the test?

Colleen Keywood

UNWANTED LOVE

Before love moved in, my mind was stable, rational, sensible and predictable.

Then love knocked at the door and I welcomed it with open arms, like a long lost friend

It soon took over and turned my life upside down. I was a slave to love, swept away on an emotional tidal wave.

Then, finally, you told me my love was unrequited.

I felt like I'd been hit by a bus, had not foreseen this outcome.

Now I want love to leave so that I can continue with my life. But, all requests are met with refusal. Don't know if it will ever leave.

Anger is rife now. Anger with myself for being so gullible, for wasting so much time and energy, for allowing it in so easily. Anger with you for not being brave enough to tell me my love was unrequited a long time ago.

It is making my life a misery, causing so much heartache, unhappiness and despair. I feel like I am falling apart.

If only I could hate you it would help but, no, I can't, not while love is there.

But, I am much harsher now and, if love ever comes knocking again, I will slam the door firmly in its face because my emotional health could not deal with another visit from love . . .

Nash

My Darling Wife

You pick me up when I feel down
You pull me up when I fool around
You teach me new things every day
And look after me in your special way
A fool I'd be to let you go
What I'd do, I'll never know.

You cook and clean, work your fingers to the bone
Just to make ours, a happy home
I know the kids can make you cry
So I'll be here to wipe your eye
I'll try to help out a whole lot more
So that your hands don't get so sore

I know I've been soft when the kids play up
So I'll have to try harder to avoid a big ruck
You are the last person that I want to make cry
Because you are the person that makes us get by
You are a mum, of whom we are all proud
And if we lost you, our lives it would cloud.

So we'll try to try harder and give you a rest
To prove to you that you are the best
Without you in it, our lives would be bad
And I know that without you we would be sad
So here's to a new start for us and for you
I know we can make it, because we love you too.

Jeremy Marriott

MAKE BELIEVE...

A magical ride on a carpet, high above in the sky.
Winging our way to adventure with no one to ask us, 'Why?'

We could soar overhead with a purpose, engulfed in a feeling of mirth,
and enjoy the high-flying sensation, 'til we had to come down to Earth.

Adventures are there for the taking, if only we had the nerve.
We could save a fair maiden from danger, or find us a sovereign
to serve!

With our trusty steed (who is ancient), in fact he's an old Labrador...
We would vanquish the foe in an instant - no one could ask us for more!

Our armour is made from Mum's saucepans, and our visor is just
an old sieve -
but with our bold hearts it's exciting - and we find it so hard
to believe...

... that we cannot recapture the pleasure of the knights in the days
of yore
as they jousted with lances on horseback and fell with a thud
to the floor!

In our make-believe world we are champions, there's nothing that we
cannot do.
So all day as we play we try hard in our way - to make all our dreams
come true.

Maureen Ayling

AUGUST 4TH 1914

Was it really ninety years ago that
Ignorance ended abruptly and the world imploded?
That we stood, young and eager to
Watch the storm of Satan's wrath well up

That we clamoured in awe to
Witness the devastation of his lightning and thunder,
Pressing up against the glass of life
Lest we missed it all pass by

And go it did . . .

Taking thousands of young men to
Fall as drops in that thirsty metal rain:
Thousands, thousands of old men saw
The harvest rendered, cut down, never returned

Left untended when the storm was broken
Little remains of where the hail stones once pitted
But here, in the minds of the crop, nine
Decades have gone since they smote the land

* * *

Ninety years since the crosses started,
Names scoured into hearts as well as wood;
Branded, tattooed with the pen of 'Survivor's Guilt'
Others, still crushed by ghosts desperate for home . . .

S J Robinson

LIFE'S RAINBOW

Have you stopped to think of the colours all aglow
That journey through life with us to form our own rainbow?
The cloudless days of childhood when skies seem always blue
No worries then - beyond ourselves, and friendships being true.

Those special years of growing up, when all was in its pink
And being told by elders - that of others we should think!
The early days of marriage, when all seemed to be serene
Our love, our life before us - oh how our world seemed green.

And then days tinged with sadness, when life seemed grey and black
We yearned to change our rainbow and turn our time clock back.
The warm, sweet days so mellow, with our partners we could share
Our sunsets tinged with yellow - and for once we stand and stare
And ponder at life's meaning. How did we walk that road
To reach our glorious golden days - yet learn to bear life's load?

At the end of every rainbow, 'tis said there's a pot of gold
Just waiting for us to find it - at least so I've been told.
My pot of gold my love, is you who gave me love and care
And taught me to cherish happiness: thank you for being there.

E Winifred Garland

THE BUTCHER

And the man they once
Called 'The Butcher'
Hung up his blades
And black stocking mask
For a caravan in Skegness
And somebody to love
And when the police
Finally caught him
His wife softly said;
'My husband, oh dear
you must have the wrong man.
He was always so gentle,
honest and kind.
His skin smelt of almonds
and his kisses like wine.
Not my poor Davey,
you must have the wrong man.'
Nobody's that perfect,
thought the policeman.

Mark Vanner

LIFE'S REFLECTIONS

When I look into the mirror, the face that I do see
Never in a thousand years, is the girl I used to be.
Once, I was happy, I'd sparkle like champagne,
Bubble from the inside, clearly feel no pain.

Yes. I'd be the Jean Val Jean, hold out my hand and ca
Never turn a blind eye, and be cruel like Monsieur Javert
But now the mirror has shattered, there's shards upon the floor.
I have lost the will for living, there's no purpose anymore.

All the dreams I'd planned for, are shattered and forlorn.
Now there has come a time, when I wish I'd not been born.
So I look up to the heavens and offer up a prayer,
Could anybody listen, is somebody there?

God, I know you have a waiting list, and are a very busy man,
But I have a massive problem, and need a helping hand.
Now as I cast my eyes downwards to the shards upon the floor,
I see a flicker of a light, an opening of a door.

Oh yes, there must be changes, that I clearly see
The evidence is obvious, it's entirely up to me.
But there upon reflection on which was once my life,
I have known my share of trouble, sorrow joy and strife.

God didn't really bless me with notoriety or wealth.
But the greatest gift He gave me
Was the grace to be myself.

Lynda Fordham

FRIENDS

A while ago I lost my wife
But with these friends I have coped with life
So if anyone is in any doubt
They should turn to friends to help them out

But have you ever thought out loud
When you are caught out in a crowd?
Do you feel lonely? Do you intend
To look around to see if you can see a friend?

Someone to talk to who will understand
If you feel lost, to take your hand
Everyone needs someone like this
A friend that they would always miss

Me, I am lucky, I have friends like these
There are others who would talk just to please
Just think a while as thoughts embrace
As friends they make mine a welcome face
One does not need to know that is true
It's nice to know they care for you

So next time you think someone turns on the charm
Do not greet it with a look of false alarm
Just stop and think like everyone
With friends like these I am the lucky one
I do not name them, that is plain
But if they are genuine, what's in a name?

E W Hockley

STREET STRUMMER

A silent street strummer,
Works the guitar,
Goes through the motions,
Thoughts seem far,
Away.

Folk walk by,
Few drop a coin,
And wonder why,
The guitar gives no sound.
Inscrutable, the musician,
Just watches the ground.

Those passing by,
Cannot know,
In a long gone day,
With that musician,
Great talent lay.

Barbara Robinson

THE ROBIN

Radiant robin with splendid colour
Amidst a carpet white with snow
And with a fire-like breast of red
Stands out so in the snow.

Have you seen his tiny legs
And his dainty little feet?
Don't you think he is sweet?

Amy Barrett

MAY RESULT IN SERIOUS AILMENT

I am a *super bug*.
I won't tell you my name, but there is a clue in the title.
I am strong and resilient, whilst you humans are puny and weak.
You shiver and die each time I speak.
I've been around since the beginning of time,
So why do you perceive my existence as a crime?
After all, you go to war, causing famine and pestilence.
And millions die!
Yet, when I kill a few thousand, you start to cry!
Well, I ask you!
You just can't see sense!
Millions die at colossal expense.
And you want to destroy me?

Steve Friede

REGRETS

You came
with your
easy charm

Plucking
at my
heart strings

Too soon to be
submerged
I turn
away

Alone,
I ponder
and regret.

D M Burnett

Green Spaces

I like to see a woodland scene.
Different shades of brown and green!
See a majestic trunk on a tall tree,
Roots spread around on the ground to see!
Feel the warmth of the sun and gentle breeze,
Find a seat to sit on and take my ease!
Fields and hedges in my view,
With paths that lead to pastures new!
This can be found in the county of Derbyshire,
The forest woodlands are planted here!
In this area called Swadlincote,
Near where I live, not very remote!
There is hope and joy in this area today,
A place to ponder and relax, come what may.
In the hustle and bustle of this life here,
Thank God for this area in Derbyshire.

Joyce Hallifield

A Summer Day In May

Walking through the meadows on a summer's day
seeing buttercups and daisies on a day in May
the sun is shining brightly, the breeze is warm and calm,
walking through the meadows the lambs were out to play,
their mothers watching over them, by their side they stayed,
buttercups and daisies, little lambs at play,
strolling through the meadow on a summer's day in May.

Georgette Poole

WILL I RETURN?

5am, no movement from the other side
Who knows what they feel inside
Are they frightened, who's to know?
Or just like us no fear must show.

There's time for a letter, could be my last
I've felt this way many times in the past
But always lived through fear and pain
To wake next day, to fight again.

Been out three months in Flanders fields
Pushing daily forward but no side yields
Surrounded by ghosts of absent friends
Who gave their lives for war to end.

Waiting for the whistle blow
Then into no-man's-land we'll go
Shouting, screaming, terrified
Stepping over them that's died.

Could this be the last I'll see
Of blood and death surrounding me?
But even if I'm hit today
Till dark in no-man's-land I'll lay
When guns fall silent they'll come for me
For hospital or mortuary

Surrounded by my fallen brothers
Home to England and waiting mothers
Will she receive me in wooden box?
Or with missing limbs, no need for socks!
So when they ask you, 'What's it all for?
That's brought this world to bitter war?'
Tell them 'Be quiet,' and they should go
How can you answer? 'I don't know!'

Daniel Moore

WASTE? - OR RESOURCE

The choice is yours - it has to be,
Or will you pollute the sward
But need that be, it's plain to see,
One's waste is another's reward.
Recycle that you no longer need,
It's materials for which others plead;
In many ways you can assist,
Saving water with just a twist;
Or maybe returning to the earth
Rich compost for your garden's worth,
Cardboard or paper will save the trees,
By doing this you're sure to please;
Reuse glass, in many hues,
While plastic waste, they won't refuse;
Green garden waste, it is perceived
At many depots will be received;
Shredding will a mulch provide
More to put out on the side;
Milk bottle tops and old stamps
Both welcomed in other camps,
Their value many a sufferer relieves:
Kitchen waste and autumn leaves,
The choice is wide: it's there to see,
Pollute or reuse, that's the decree,
So why not let your voice endow
To shout it aloud - recycle, now,
Then let us all a vow to take
To limit our landfill, and make
The environment to conserve,
Surely that's the least we deserve.

George Beckford

The Fox

As the sun begins to set, the light begins to fade;
you come out of the shadows looking for a bin to raid.

Walking quickly across the silent road,
you prowl cautiously as your hunger grows.

No matter what the weather, you go out every night trying to survive,
doing anything to find some food before the sun begins to rise.

Nothing deters you, not even the cats,
you pass them by preferring the local mice and rats.

When the weather is sunny and warm,
you will find a quiet spot and lie stretched out on the lawn.

A wild and cunning nature you possess,
but a creature of beauty and amazement in what we see best.

Wendy Coulson

The Truth

The truth is a friend who has two faces,
So when you look into their eyes the dust clears in your heart,
It can also feel like a room,
Without a door or a floor or walls or ceiling,

If I write in blood will that make you see the rainbows
in my eyes?

But in poisoning a ghost is like writing a letter without words,
Drinking the tears from my childhood,

I can pick up the hands of time and write a smile.
The colours in my eyes are the shame of someone's voice.

Mark Anthony Allibon

AXE OF SEDUCTION

Running rhythm,
A game of chase,
You reach for my neck,
I fret as you pace.
The vibratory tones
Of pressure imposed,
Striking chords,
The melody flows.
The bridge of tension,
Pulling on strings,
Rising scales,
The pleasure it brings.
To surface ride
With finger tips,
Played with menace
Of emotional trip.

Sue Umanski

GANGSTER PRETEND INCORPORATED

Baseball caps with logo signs
mapping out a crew's territory.
Pseudo-ghetto graffiti rhymes
chiming in Siamese vainglory.
Wearing an aroma of skunk,
white boys speak fake Jamaican.
Selling goodies; chomping junk,
acting like a 'real' American.
Macho fighting out on the booze,
attacking those seen as fools.
Baleful eyes primed to abuse
non-conformity to their rules.

Billy Shears

THE DARK VISITOR

When all about me began to fall,
The visitor made his call.
The devil himself made me fall,
His words turned me upside down,
The Bible's he showed me all.
Plates of stone stood in uniform,
All religions, no difference in them all.
When death looked me in the face,
My life I wanted to take.
He showed me that it would still go on,
No escape for anyone.
I hung onto my very last breath,
I came back and escaped death.
But still I wonder what went wrong,
To make the darkness call at all.
Still in the shadows I know he lurks,
So I must always stay alert.

Anne Rickard

ODE TO KEATS

'Twas long ago, before barcodes,
When JK penned his many odes.
Loads of odes and other ditties,
Stirring thoughts, inciting pity.
Tales of love and tales of evil,
Couched in language medieval.
Tales of ancient gods and fairies,
Psyche, Prosperine and Hermes.
You didn't realise long gone scribe,
How your ancient diatribe
Would stir deep thoughts and some unrest
In this modern reader's breast.

Maureen Woodward

JOLLY JIHAD

I think: if only we didn't bother
With cases,
Then, the Immigration Man
(as only they can
At present) looks and sees
Something that he shouldn't have.
'Take a look at this!'
You ask, 'Is that mine?' and
'Can I help?'
'That way. That way.'
We're moved along the line.
'Keep moving.'

I could have said that it's
A camera gone shy
Among the clothes. Maybe.

Rippling through the queue
Of incomers disconnected,
American official smiles,
Surprised! You coming here
On holiday? And pleased.
How much is politics a war of nerves?
How much it serves them ill?
They can't direct
A single step
Ahead.
But dream they're through the wars.
Peace elect.
Do you believe it?
On your head be it.

Diane Burrow

ME BIKE'S GOT A PUNCTURE!

Me bike's got a puncture!
And the tyres are wearin' thin,
'But it's not from all that skiddin','
I says with a cheeky grin.
Me back wheel's got a buckle,
And I know I've got no brakes,
But I love this little bike o' mine,
When I'm ridin' with me mates.
The handlebars are loose,
They keep turning to the side,
But I just think it helps,
Make a more interestin' ride.
And every time I do me jump,
Me seat comes off its post,
And when I'm flyin' through the air,
Me friends wet themselves the most.
Even when I've hurt meself,
They roll around the floor,
Chucklin' and gigglin'
And laugin' even more.
It's no good getting angry,
Cos I love me little bike,
And even with all its faults,
It's better than me trike.
So I never think I'll change it,
And even if I do,
Me bike will always 'ave a puncture,
Even if it's new!

Tony Pratt

A Christmas Parcel

I am a Christmas parcel, in red and green I'm dressed,
With a ribbon round my middle and a bow tied round my neck.
No one knows what's inside, except the careful packer,
I've tried to shake myself to see, but it's hard, so does it matter?

What does the label say? Let's look, oh it's for Auntie Suzy,
Now she's a lady of renown and always is quite choosey.
So let us think what it might be, but we mustn't let her know,
Just one more shake, then have a guess; we've got to have a go.

Am I heavy? No I'm not, so packing must be plenty,
You don't suppose it's all a joke and I am really empty?
What does Auntie Suzy like? I know she likes a drink,
I've seen her in the kitchen; she hides it by the sink!

She dresses well, to hide the fat! But don't let's even think of that!
Perhaps a corset, to keep her in? She'd never squeeze into it
                                            after the gin.
She does like her chocolate, as clearly it does show,
But by the fire I've sat all week, I'd have melted by the glow!

I wonder who the parcel's from? That might give us a clue,
'Happy Christmas Auntie Suzy, with love from next door's *Boo*'.
Now Boo's a dog, how can he wrap a parcel such as me?
I bet he's got this owner Tom to do the dirty deed.
Now Tom's a man who likes a joke, so that some help might give,
Auntie Suzy's not so keen on all he does, or did!

He smokes a bit of weed you see and sometimes gets quite high,
A social afternoon with Tom, she was floating in the sky.
It's time to have another think, now what else can it be?
I've done my best, can't work it out, we'll have to wait and see.

A few more days to go until my contents are revealed,
Until that time I'll have to sit, all tied and bowed and sealed.
Aunt Suzy will my ribbon cut and rip the wrapping free,
Until that time I'll have to sit, under the Christmas tree.

Eileen Thomas Davies

AFTER TEA! JAMES SAID

My niece collected James, aged five,
Said to him, 'Today my office asked for help,
Need toys or money to keep children alive.
Poorly African boys starving and sick,
No mummies or daddies to buy them games,
I promised to take some in tomorrow,
Don't you agree James?'
'Oh yes Mummy, we'll do it after tea!'
Mummy contradicted, 'It takes time!
Sort those to stay and those to go, tomorrow they'll be
                                        shipped overseas.'
My niece remarked encouragingly, 'Walk to and fro.
Play that's for you and that's for me.'
James was frowning, puzzlingly,
Protesting, 'I thought we were going to send
Piles and piles and piles of Marmite sandwiches?'
Standing tiptoe, hands reaching skywards.
'James, you must have lots of spare toys if you rummage.'
'Alright Mummy, I'll look through my toy box.'
His legs stretched utmost to climb steep stairs,
She thought, *a good boy and to be candid,*
He rarely plays with toys from earlier years;
In her own mind she knew he wouldn't return empty-handed.
Later, James descended slowly his arms full,
Socks rolled around his ankles, grinning ear to ear.
'Look Mummy! Lots and lots for lots of games.'
'I must say your room must look clear,
You've done very well, James.'
Thinking; *like all men, James, you have to be prised*
From your gadgets, games and toys,
Women have to bear in mind, never to be surprised
No matter, the age boys will forever be boys!

Hilary Jill Robson

GALAXY

Our scorching sun burns brightly in the twilight sky,
Breathing life into the only abode we know,
The solar system, like nine lost marbles waiting to be claimed,
But who can claim them? Not you or I.

Mercury, taking the brunt of the gas giant's anger,
Venus, a mysterious beauty, too humid to explore,
Mars, the Martian base according to myth.

An asteroid belt gives shape to the abyss.

Jupiter, the gentle giant commands the second wave,
Saturn, sports dazzling rings and a body to envy,
Uranus, a mimic of Saturn's promise yet still unique,
Neptune, an ocean of bitterness and freezing winds,
Pluto, Neptune's cousin in need of a friend.

And then there's Earth, the best of all, where humans rule
supreme yet they remain vulnerable.

Stuart Feek (15)

A FORGOTTEN PART OF ENGLAND

There's a forgotten part of England in the Chilterns' chalky soil,
Where men with giant excavators and backs of brown have toiled,
They've swallowed up this mighty field to keep the kiln house
burning chalk,
to build another cement town on another field of chalk.

Yet, not a stone's throw from this very works, the quarry's wound
runs deep,
though its edges are healed by hawthorn and its base with its weep.
But to see it now with its evergreens and crystal-clear lake,
It's a forgotten part of England, an industrial mistake . . .

Martyn Suddaby

COMMON KNOWLEDGE

Life in the House of Commons is real, just like the security scare
we had that day.
How do those distinguished silver-tongued guides remember their
word-perfect running commentary?
Queen Elizabeth l, Queen Victoria, and King Edward VIII deck
the Halls of Fame.
Exposé of their lives adorn the walls just like 'OK' magazine.
The gold leaf designs, attention to detail and craftsmanship throughout
are amazing.
With portraits painted directly onto stone walls and framed
for posterity, definitely not for the taking.
One group after the other, herded through hallowed corridors
and chambers.
We cannot tarry for we have an 'audience' with our local MPs,
How nice, is that where we persuade them to lobby in our favour?

Alas, our time is limited our burning questions put on hold,
Lunch is to be served and we must be seated for our meal of roast pork
with crackling, apple sauce and mash, followed by crème brûlée -
I'm sold!

After lunch, a quick visit to the shop to buy a memento for posterity
With obligatory key ring in hand, surely there's time for the
honourable privy!

We congregate once more to finish off our tour,
It's been a great day at the House of Commons and certainly not a bore.
And whilst the debate continues about public access to this day,
My vote, you've guessed, is a resounding - 'Aye, aye!'

Mea Tate

DREAMS OF THE HEART

Hardly ever a day goes by that I don't think of you,
and wonder how your arms would feel around me very tight,
and your heart beating close to mine in harmony and love,
your tender lips so sweet on mine,
your smile like sunshine warm.

To walk together hand in hand
through meadows full of flowers sweet,
and ride white horses through the surf
on some deserted beach.

But oh! These things can never be,
they're only dreams within my heart,
just longings of a yearning soul,
a love that I can never show,
except in lonely dreams.

Sheila Giles

WINTER REARS ITS UGLY HEAD

As winter rears its ugly head,
The world around looks bare and dead.
Storm clouds make the sky dark and grey,
It feels as if night lasts all day.

The snow is hiding blades of grass,
Water shines like plates of glass.
Icicles hang from every branch,
Wildlife seems to have little chance.

But spring will come and life is reborn,
Emerging safely from winter's scorn.
When all things start to live and thrive,
And you can again see a world that is bright and alive.

Paul Clarke

FANTASY

Lonely night warns of a coming fright
I can tell time has a twist to bring
A twist to leave me shivering
And broken as I am
I sense more to come!
Sense I'm far from done
The lazy legs
The lazy body
Tell of a shattered soul
But still, here am I
Broken and bruised
Drained of blood
Life sprinting away
But not defeated!

Oh sweet dark night
Hide the sun so bright
Come rescue me
Take me to sleep
Where nought can touch me
Only the silence of my mind
To heal my broken flesh
And what can save me?
Only to be elsewhere
Somewhere away from me
Somewhere away from here
But in my sleep I dread the day
For torment comes in the day
Slowly slithering my way
Saying nothing will be okay
Sweet night come take me away.

Emmanuel Ntezeyombi

WINTER GLASS

Outside cold comfort a stranger waits
For emptiness on the road to escape.

The confusion of what to do after your dreams
Have led you dancing through a magical fog
Then cleared leaving you in an unfamiliar town.

A place of dying roads leading to Hell
And nobody said you had to pick one.

Even signposts are frank about dead passions
As they are beaten gradually blank by powerful winds
And rain that gets heavier as years peel off and fade.

What use have the teacher's ghostly voices now?
Nothing but articulate words and stale coffee breath!

Elders holding the child's hand to the end of the street
Then letting go and vanishing into the sinister city mist
A growing mind left alone amongst rubbish and ugly buildings.

A sudden shock of money grabbing frenzy
Sours the soul away from truth and destiny.

Then a chill breeze shivers away warm ambitions
On the promise of a refreshing relationship with God
Because death seems to close in like storm clouds.

Suddenly age whispers gradually over our skin
Leaving empty lines for some unwritten story.

All that can be said and done disappears
Into some thin memory which frosts over
Leaving winter glass and broken dreams.

Only good people can wither without remorse
Leaving bad apples joining the queue for selfish ends.

Only youth keeps the glowing candle alight
Leaving, eventually, a statue of old lifeless wax.

Bobby-Joe Parker

A DREAM

When I close my eyes I see
A word unspoken
A tune unsung
And a morning unbroken
So does everyone

Like tomorrow isn't there
When you reach out for a dream
It turns into thin air
Or that is what it seems

You want to keep it in your mind
You want to hold it in your heart
But you know you will never find
That ever distant part

Because everyone has fears
Because every single one
Has laughed, smiled and shed tears
And a dream is just life's fun

Alice Tarran Banks (10)

MOTHER

You taught me to talk
Aided me to walk
Kissed me goodnight
Reassured me everything will be alright.
Read me stories
Of fairies' glories
Sang me lullabies and folk songs
Waved me off to school
By your side, against the fireside
You taught me many skills to fill time.
But in my teens, no reasoning, no rhyme
Tragedy struck my life,
Ill you became, lost the strife
And eventually you died.
From that day, everyday, tears I have cried.
For me now, no mother to share
The trials of womanhood.
Without you my soul is bare,
My misery has never been understood.
As you died, severed were the special ties
Between mother and daughter.
Now in heavenly skies
My guardian angel you are
Watching over me from afar.

Elaine Hicklin

YOUTH

He was thoughtless, reckless and without a care
Only to me did he turn when in despair
Look after me and treat me well
Then I will love you from Heaven to Hell

His thoughts were for himself alone
Unable to give himself from heart to bone
Vulnerable to the outside world
Wanting life to give him a chance

But are you happy in your youthful age
Or once again are you living in a cage
A cage of narrow-mindedness
Thoughts for only yourself

A shell of a person with no depth
Is an existence all you require
Live for today with not a care for tomorrow
Pleasure is there for you to borrow

One of these tomorrows will bring sorrow
With no one to share the last of your years
And who will you turn to in your old age
You will be alone in your self made cage

Kathryn E Needham

SHINE ON (A BALLAD)

Summer sun has just began
A beginner, the rays just ran
Deep in the heart of man
The clock on the wall
Children at the dodgems and stalls
Everything you do
You want to give up the cash
Housewife's bangers and mash
You have to earn your nosh
Sorry kids - turned up smiles
Party crackers shine on in piles
The doc won't stop
Shifting laxative with sena and pop
But you can't do without a prop
Theatrical - and a croc
Watch the back step
I just can't enough
Money is so tough
Now I am on the street duff, duff, dosh
I try to be alone but people just swarm.

Hardeep Singh-Leader

TRAIN JOURNEY

Blades of grass rushing by inground circles
Sheep stand feeding, enjoying God's lush gifts
Barns rusting, shades of blue floating on green
Boasting rich colours the long-necked creature
Beautiful, elegant garden keeper
Bursts of heather blended with lavender
Water flows down racing against nature
Milk beasts grey and soft, hints of creamy-white
Multitudes of colours in harmony
Lily pads silently harbouring frogs
Solitary cottage, never lonely
Reeds hide the expanse of flowing waters
Sleepy harbour, still dark and lifeless
Twisted and deformed branches bare no light
Water falls between hills bathed in yellow
Droplets whip the rocks hidden under green
Behind the window, nature has no smell
Scents of pine attempt to reach the senses
Beams of light like tunnels through undergrowth
Cities hide nature's secrets underground
Covered by concrete, never to be found.

Beverley Morton

SHAME ON ME

Over and under, few and far between.

I found you, then lost you,
trying to make sense of it all.

Shame on me for losing myself,
for handing you a heart worth breaking.
Shame on me, as I free fall in my bittersweet kaleidoscope,
spinning around into beautiful oblivion.

Over and under, few and far between.

Standing alone in the night a silent moon hears my cry,
and mirrors my heart, once full now waning into nothing.

Shame on me for giving myself so completely,
for wanting only love in return.
Shame on me, as I watch you leave my side forever,
tearing my soul into a myriad of pieces.

Over and under, few and far between . . .

Kate Ransom

IN THE EYE OF THE BEHOLDER

Little Jimmy stands and watches
Mummy's face, in creamy blotches,
Mascara, lipstick and facial blusher
All serve his question in to usher

A simple question - he's only four,
'Mummy, what's all that stuff for?'
Mummy turns from dressing table
Ready to answer as best she's able

'Well, my little cutieful,
It's all to make Mummy beautiful
Just for you, my little chappie
And to keep your daddy happy.'

As he maintains his observations
Now hangs a threat to their good relations
The fateful question he does not shirk
'Mummy, when's it going to work?'

Brian Ford-Powell

THE POWER OF THE WORD

Reading is about escape, into the lives of familiar faces
Or to travel, to far exotic places.
From village to town, to city to nation,
The only limit is your imagination.

Imagination becomes thought, thought becomes writing,
That's when things get really exciting.
Be it pen to paper, or fingers to keys,
Your mind holds a world of possibilities.

Anything is possible in poetry, prose or song,
But when all else fails there's conversation,
Phone calls, discussions, conferences and meetings
Are no more important than simple greetings.

Do not give up on words, read, write and talk when you can,
For this is the truth for every woman and man:
When words are lost, when they go away,
What will happen to the things you want to say?

Daniel Adams

AFTER SHE'S GONE
(Dedicated to my mum)

They stand alone upon a bridge,
They stand over water,
They stand as one within their hearts,
The mother and the daughter.

They remember the good times,
Gone and slipped away,
They look at each other,
And what they are today.

The times they spent together,
Are slowly going to end,
The mother and the daughter,
Turn another bend.

But now she's gone,
Like a lamb to the slaughter,
But the good times to stay,
From the mother and her daughter.

Teri Manning (11)

MY NATURAL HIGH

Just the other day,
I felt something quite unique.
Will you please listen to me while I say
About this extraordinary feeling I wish to re-seek

You see, for a while I've been feeling low
Adolescence, I guess, your normal negativity
What with exams, revision, and so
Compressed stress, depression, kept quietly

I often think it's not worth my while
No prospects or goals nor ambitions or dream
I'm a spectator, drifting - but suicide? Nah, it's not my style
But this rare occurrence - a natural high, it happened to me,
                                   and for a reason, so it seems

That's why I want to share it with you
The experience that opened my eyes
I saw the light. You know, I still don't have a clue
There are no answers, the future's no clearer, but somehow
                                   it still made me realise

I still don't understand
And nothing's in context in my head
Joyful ecstasy I can't explain. Take my hand
And just hold on until one day when you will feel it too
Then you'll see what it is that drives you every morning
                                   to get out of bed

Anya Lees

KINGFISHERS

A kingfisher perched
On a willow by the brook,
And while my eager eyes searched
A kingfisher perched
Near where I slowly lurched
Near for a closer look
A kingfisher perched
On a willow by the brook

I could only dream
Of kingfishers on my farm
And it would seem
I could only dream
As no trees overlooked the stream
Though I come to no harm
I could only dream
Of kingfishers on my farm

Forty years on
I saw kingfishers again
When the trees had gone
Forty years on
They were sitting on
A house roof in the rain
Forty years on
I saw kingfishers again

Dan Pugh

SEASIDE

On the beach spitting waves aspire
Fall upwards, swish, higher and ever higher
Pebbles slide away. A seagull sulks among dunes
Flies up into the cobalt blue sky making shrill tunes

The fish sink heavily beneath a tall wave
Waiting it seems to see who's brave
Among the seaweed tiny creatures dart
Caught on rocks and clammy dull sand they start

Windsurfers slip into view and out again
Ever patient in turbulence they strain
Grimly holding on to defy balance
For a second, then drop like lemmings in dance

At sea someone flashes by on water skis
Across the ocean he glides, turns and hurries
Back into view. Golden sun shines high above
Children sniff sea air, play in yellow ochre sand in the cove

Various dogs walk by. Then people pack up - leave for home
One after another. Some linger and roam
Behind is left the debris of another Sunday
Papers, packets, bottles, colour the rich array

Night arrives, the waves quieten and gently lap at designs
Of sandcastles long forgotten. Peace and calm reigns.

Sheila Cheesman

RIVER SEVERN

Where goes the canoeist paddling by?
Is he idling as I am under fluffy sky?
Water gently flowing not a ripple showing
Except where his paddles make circling
Patterns of rhythm in the quietly breathing
River Severn

Britain's longest river aspires
To course its way through several shires
An amenity for boating and fishing fraternity
Sightseers of glee, ornithology and botany
Reaping the joys of the moodily mighty
River Severn

Flood peaks are its fearful detraction
Providing attraction by such distraction
Devastation at times to people frenetic
Thought, deed and act become energetic
Spearing effort to tame a sorely splenetic
River Severn

If a picture tells ten thousand words
Calm river reflections gain double rewards
Camera computer combine to quadruple
And introduce with scarcely a scruple
A verbose snapshot of a very beautiful
River Severn

P A Findlay

MY UNCLE'S DYING

My uncle's dying and I don't know what to do
My teddy bear's the only one I can talk to
Just seeing my uncle there
So poorly in intensive care
Makes me feel so sad
Because my uncle's really bad
I wish it was me instead
All he does is doze in bed
I go to the hospital nearly every day
It's a long journey, but I need to stay
Close, he got over his operation
There was not one complication
He's getting better but refusing to eat
I really don't want his heart not to beat
I love him dearly you see, I don't want him to die
Someday soon, I'm sure he'll get by

Rebecca Smith (12)

BLUE SEA

Swimming in the rich blue sea
Underneath little crabs running around
Also jellyfish can be found
Moving arms and legs to keep afloat
Mind the little children paddling about
Each time you float, try and relax
So as your body not to tax
Then run up and down the seashore
This you will like, that is for sure.

Garry Bedford

It's All Talk

Things we can see, objects that surround us,
We believe because we can see.
We cannot see the air around us
Yet we know and believe it is there.
So to believe means one must see,
Or one must have evidence in order to distinguish the truth.
Then what about a story that we are told?
People we have never met or known,
Events in words and nothing beyond,
Believed without being tested.
We treat every word
As gospel and truth.

The faces of people with whom are involved in the words
Accused of being the subject of truth,
Feel the lies and falsehood these words hold,
The stab of pain each one contains.

So why do we believe these words
Without seeing, observing or witnessing?
We take each word and make them real to us,
Create our own pictures in our own minds
From the fiction that we hear.
The visual evidence cannot be found
Yet still we proceed to believe.
To believe what we can see or is proved
Is a theory we place to the side
As these words we hear, or read, or say
Are more exciting and interesting
Than the actual truth.

So when words are passed through any medium
About who we are not and where we have not been,
Minds of others will believe as did we,
And we will feel what others have felt, the
Mindless gossip, which causes the pain.

Emily Watts

BEING YOU

Good times, bad times
Smiles and tears
Joy and laughter
Worry and fears

It's life, it's living
It's who we are
The stage is set
For us to play our part

What is our role?
What character do we play?
Why are we here?
What do we say?

Am I the lead
Or am I backstage?
Should I be here
Is this my stage?

Knowing our role
On this great stage of life
Will prepare and protect us
From the pitfalls and strife

Our role is vital
No other can play it
We've been hand-picked by God
To rise up and fulfil it

He's formed us and shaped us
To do the things that we do
Maybe it's lead, maybe it's backstage
But most important is just, being you.

Trevor Brammah

THE DEATH OF DC OAKE

Nobody thought he would die,
As he helped the country doing his job,
Nobody thought that he would be killed
By an angry terrorist mob.

One grotty January evening,
He left three kids and a wife,
And went out to call at a flat,
Where he received his death with a knife.

His family mourned yesterday,
Crying out their grief,
They wrote their messages down on paper,
And called the murderer a thief.

The dead constable's father, Robin,
And his wife, Christine Oake,
Laid down their tribute of red roses,
Choking back the tears in their throats.

His children laid down flowers,
They held their faces so brave,
As the rain thundered down,
Hitting their father's grave.

To the funeral came Police Officer Todd,
Who made formal enquiries at the end.
But he had also come to say goodbye,
To his very faithful friend.

Nobody thought he would die,
As he helped the country doing his job,
Nobody thought that he would be killed,
By an angry terrorist mob.

Lianne Kemp (14)

Slowing Down

Just talking to a chap one day,
Who some might call a friend.
It seems he's living aimlessly,
Just waiting for the end!
His eyesight isn't what it was,
His hearing seems impaired,
For some time now he's lived alone,
I asked him how he fared?
Just recently he'd had a fall,
Which didn't help his sight,
He's only got one good eye,
Which underlines his plight!
In years, he's getting on a bit,
Well past three score and ten,
But still he walks to town each day,
I applaud him with my pen.
So many senior citizens,
Live longer, feeling young,
Recalling all their yesterdays,
Things, that they have done.
For some of them, however,
Old bodies feel the strain,
And many things they long to do,
Can no longer entertain.
In this modern age of medicine,
It's the pills that do the trick,
In truth we're living longer,
Though we can't move quite so quick.

T G Bloodworth

Books

Books in the window, books on the floor,
Books near the ceiling, books near the door.

I can go to rainforests and watch a waterfall,
I can defeat bad guys and go shopping in a mall.

I can fly on an eagle's back,
I can escape from a haunted shack.

I can be a spy,
And nearly die.

I can wrestle a wild boar,
I can knock down a castle door.

I could solve a murder
And put the culprit in jail,
I could go to another world
With the help of a giant whale.

But what is really cool
Is I started from a chair,
And by the time I've read those books
I'm still sitting there!

Connor Law (10)

JUDGEMENT

Here I am on Judgement day
Almighty God, He had His way
The world is gone, there is but clouds
And now I'm staring at the crowd
They cry and moan and beg and scream
Praying it's a nasty dream
A dream it is not, we all are forgot
We have one life and that's your lot
As the angels fall before us all
Some begin to smile, some brawl
Yet most of them have similar fate
They all end up at devil's gate
Burning, starving, coughing blood
Forever pain whilst in the mud
But here I am waiting in strife
The call to say what I did in my life
When it finally comes there's a sense of relief
Knowing I'll never get to see their chief
'So what have you done?' they ask in the best
I look around to check the rest
Some speak of good, the others just wailed
I simply replied, I tried, and failed

Benjamin Puyenbroek

WEATHER REPORT

Lancashire have had a shower
It poured all day long hour by hour
It was so bad
That I'm very glad
I'm in Blackpool on top of the tower

In Yorkshire I am told there is hail
I can't really believe half this tale
The speaker just garbles
The stones are like marbles
My imagination at this will just fail

In London they're suffering snow
The streets are really 'no go'
The cars are all jammed
The stations are crammed
I hope by July it will go

Five thousand campers in Devon
Thought they're in a state next to Heaven
Until torn right asunder
By lightning and thunder
Now they are reduced down to seven

In the Midlands the weather is fine
My washing is out on the line
My sunburn is sore
I can't take much more
So I'll sit in the shade until nine

R W Meacheam

MY SPECTACLES TO ANYWHERE

My much loved, reading glasses
Seem to be nothing spectacular,
Yet they allow me to see different worlds.
Having eye appeal, they are scene-stealers,
Which I use so freely to explore.
With Lyra in Philip Pullman's 'Dark Trilogy'
Transferring to parallel Earth's in an instant,
Or to many treasure or coral islands
And live like Daniel Defoe's lonely Crusoe.
Take long journeys to far distant stars.
I'm given to wandering ancient castles,
Or Germanic forests deep and dark,
Maybe the Great Shires of Middle Earth,
With those friendly little folk,
We've come to love, known as hobbits.
Venture down the dark burrows,
Of disarmingly charming, talking rabbits,
On the hillsides of Watership Down.
Exploring fecund, tropical jungles,
With its cannibals and fierce animals.
Slinking thru' the dank alleyways,
Of Queen Victoria's London town.
Earlier meeting good King Henry,
And his volatile, flame-haired daughter,
The 1st Queen Elizabeth of renown.
Voyage to the dim and distant past,
When great dinosaurs shook the ground.
I can't deny my glasses are wonderful,
But my ability to read, I perceive,
Is my meal ticket to anywhere.

Julia Pegg

ANOTHER NIGHT

Another night draws in
And up the stairs to bed I go
I read my book, but cannot look
For my mind is somewhere else I know
The darkness that surrounds me, it frightens me so
I look around my bedroom, and see the shape upon my walls
They look so wide, and yet so tall
My mind's playing tricks again
I look under my bed, I cannot get to sleep
I imagine monsters of all kinds hiding there
I'm scared to move, or get out of bed
So I lay my head, to try to sleep
And start to end up counting sheep.

I finally drop off
And dream of beautiful things
And big butterflies
Opening their wings
Fairies and castles
And all sorts of things
Hope my dream lasts
Until I awake in the morning
And look out of my window
And see a new day dawning.

M Woolvin

MOMMY, PLEASE, PLEASE CAN I STAY?

Oh Mommy, I keep getting this horrible pain,
Make it go away. Ouch, it's hurting me again.
Do we really have to go to the doctor's today?
I would rather go out with my mates to play.

The doctor says I have to go to hospital, why?
Mommy, does this mean I'm going to die?
I'm ever so scared; it sounds a really scary place,
Are you taking me? Will I have to take a suitcase?

Mom, there are other kids in here, just like me,
Oh look at him; he's got a bandage on his knee.
She's got a patch on her eye and her arm in a sling,
Can I have one? Why not? You never get me anything!

Look at the toys and games and pictures on the wall,
There are books and CDs. I like the PlayStation best of all.
See that nurse over there, the one with the red hair?
Well she read me a story last night about a day at the fair.

Look at my stitches. Will I have a scar? Will I be the same?
Guess what Mom? The nurses and doctors all know my name!
They said I've been brave and the nasty pain has gone away,
I like it in here. Mommy, please, can I stay?

Karen Whitehouse

WHAT I SAW

In my garden
I saw . . .

An ant,
Run up a plant,
That's not funny.

An earwig
Dance a jig,
That's not funny.

A butterfly
Flutter by,
That's not funny.

A caterpillar on his own
That crawled beneath a great big stone,
That's not funny.

But
When I picked up a *worm*
It made me squirm,
It wriggled and wriggled,
I giggled and giggled,
Now that's funny.

H S Burn

IF I WAS AN ANGEL

If I was an angel, I don't think I'd conform
For when do I ever do what is the norm?
If I was an angel, I'd decorate my wings
Sew beads and sequins in their hundreds and other shiny things
If I was an angel, I'd probably dye my hair
Red and blue and pink and green and I'd really dare
If I was an angel, I'd never clean my halo
I'd never seen a duster so that's definitely a no
If I was an angel, I'd wear a glittered gown
Because glitter is my favourite thing whenever I feel down
If I was an angel, I think I'd pierce my tongue
So if I ever aged it would help to make me still feel young
If I was an angel, I'd look down on my mother
Reminding me of how we were when we spent time together
If I was an angel, I'd smile down on my dad
I'd remember how he helped at times when I was a little bit mad
If I was an angel, I'd think of my brother Matt
I'd remember when we were young how we tormented our poor cat
If I was an angel, I'd laugh at my nan's trolley
She needs a licence to drive that thing and lessons on using her brolly
If I was an angel, I'd do things I've never done
I'd make sure I'd live a life
That was jam-packed full of fun

Sarah Streeter

THANKS

You sat beside me on stone steps
And blotted out the world.
Thanks.
You took my country house dream
and moulded it to wanderlust.
Thanks.
You saw this wretched, sobbing child
and grew her, like a flower, to a woman.
Thanks.
You gave me pride in my kisses
and a clear vision of Eros.
This is a seesaw, I'm grounded with love.
Thank you, thank you, thank you.

Catherine Boal

MY PROMISE

I will know always how cold it is without you
and I will never let pride hold me back.
I will risk everything to show you all,
because you are the beginning
and you are the end.
Eternal hope,
you are.

Lucy Bradford

EACH LITTLE SOUL

Everything comes to he who waits,
This is the story I'm told,
Tell that to the boy with the big, sad brown eyes,
Just a few grains of rice in his bowl.

Tell that to the baby who cries all alone,
In a war ravaged country, so cold,
Tell that to a mum with a babe at her breast,
Whose life milk no longer flows.

Tell that to the young girl in nightmare's hell,
As into slavery she's sold,
To abuse unthinkable, her innocence gone,
Relieved only when death takes its toll.

Tell the millions of babies starving each day,
They never will live to grow old,
I pray that the rich man will think with his heart,
And surrender a portion of gold.

Tells in the bible, not one sparrow dies,
Without our God knows of its fall,
Tells of the Heaven where all children smile,
Pure paradise for each little soul.

Everything comes to he who waits,
This is the story I'm told,
Dear Lord take the hurting, the babies, their tears,
In your safe arms of love please enfold.

Dorothy M Mitchell

A Beautiful Love

Two souls entwine
In time and space,
This wondrous day;
A golden hour;
A tender blessing
Of God's good grace
And seeds of love
Shall ever flower.
As fragrant blooms
At end of day,
As songbirds on branches high,
When sunset's rays
The heavens meet;
Our love shall never die.

Tracey Lynn Birchall

Blake Marsh

They are felling trees in Blake Marsh
Where squirrels play and birds sing,
It was here a young squirrel and I played peek-a-boo this spring.
His bright eyes peering from behind a stump,
His cheeky face with look of 'I spy'
Seen first from the grass, then from a clump.
Was it his mother watching, silhouetted against grey sky
Her bushy tail curled over her back,
Making sure no harm came to mischievous son Jack?
She had found a branch on a lone tree
And was sitting pressed against the trunk, her face hidden from me.
Lower down on the bark was painted a red mark
Clear and harsh.
They are felling trees in Blake Marsh.

N M Beddoes

HOPE

This year will be my year.
Next week shall be my week.
I'll land a job, I'll be someone.
My head I shall hold up high
And walk proudly looking at the sky.

I shall look and feel my best.
Facial features fixed forever in a smile.
There will be nothing I cannot do,
For I shall be valued and employed,
And all my fears and woes be null and void.

Yes. This year will be my year.
Next week will be my week.
I'll land the job that I've been looking for.
For hope, yes hope, is in my eye;
But hope exists: and then you die.

J G Ryder

CIRCULAR

'Brennen! Kennen! How wide your riverbed!'
The soft exposure that greeted the woebegone,
Kept close to me; keep close to the stones' mossy cover,
Lowly by reaping, hide your riverbed.

'I shall not sleep!' he uttered, shouted,
Confirmed, the newness displayed its consent,
Call near to me; call to the stones' hoary fissure,
Misting the woodland, gaping he shouted . . .

Graham Freestone

MONNIE B'

Monnie B' is a character
From where I live.
She would rather starve
Than not be able to give.

Her body though not pretty
Oozes with love,
I am sure that when she dies
She'll go up above.

Her make-up is a cross between
Tommy and Henry Cooper,
If she joined the marines
She'd be a hell of a trooper.

You really should see her
To know what I mean,
As she oozes more character
Than I've previously seen.

I see her come
And I see her go,
But of her destination
I do not know.

She's always busy
But in slow motion,
As she hasn't the speed
But she does have the notion.

I love Monnie B'
Despite her age of 79,
As she smells of parsley
Sage and thyme.

Gary Liles

Day In The Life Of A Mum

She gets up early, she feels half dead
Sticky eyes and a thumping head
Move to the bathroom for a wake up call
Steadies herself to prevent a fall

Shout the kids for them to wake
Three or four times for goodness sake
Breakfast time, tea and toast
Prepare the veg for the evening roast

Kids to school is a daily run
Rush hour traffic not much fun
Off to work for an hour or two
Return home then for more to do

Dusting here and dusting there
Hoovering up and down the stairs
Tidy this and tidy that
Not even time to stop and chat

Once the kids are home from school
She's wasted her time is the general rule
Why she bothers she doesn't know
She's cleaned the house but it doesn't show

Kids fed, bathed and put to bed
Now the job she really dreads
Ironing is her worst chore
She wouldn't care if she did no more

Eleven o'clock she gets sat down
She's really tired but there's no frown
She can't do more she gave her best
Off to bed for a hard earned rest

Neil Warren

I Was A Tulip

How I wish I was a tulip standing so straight and tall
Growing here in this garden that is far from small
As I hear the gardener's music really rocking
Apon the garden wall.

How I wish I was a tulip floating in the wind
As the gardener looks apon the leaves wondering where to begin
For they cover up many sins from the night before
Because last night there was a party here that really upset next door.

How I wish I was a tulip amongst all the other flowers
For we then could talk forever simply hour after hour
Is the water in the swimming pool still as nice and clean
Or with the leaves was something washed away
That someone else should really have seen.

Keith L Powell

Father Bus 4 Sale

Father bus for sale
Kind of good condition
Likes to go on an expedition
Runs on cakes
But doesn't know how to bake
He's my dad
But watch out he's a bit mad
Had one owner but needed a donor
If it's a race he won't come last
He's kinda fast
£2000 or nearest offer
Call 01234 I need a bus

Devon Stewart (12)

BEYOND THE RAINBOW

Beyond the rainbow, beyond the trees,
Beyond the whispering of the leaves,
There's a place for you and I -
Where there's no need to ever cry.
Higher than the birds can soar -
Is peace and solitude where you're
In charge of whom you want to be,
Higher than a scudding, ethereal cloud
Away from the roar of traffic so loud,
Is the calm we all need, strive to seek?
Available every hour of every week,
Higher still than the blue we see from Earth
A place where everyone has their worth,
It's here I go when times are tough,
When all I feel is tired and rough,
And all the postman ever brings are bills
Also, you can't live on caffeine pills.
So shut out the hustle and bustle around,
Close the door to annoying, irritating sound,
Listen with your heart, and the eyes of your soul,
Search for that world where you can be whole,
Hear the silence of peace raining down -
Let it erase those worries and that frown,
Soak in the stillness that calm can bring -
Letting go for a moment of everything,
Hear the music as a butterfly flutters along,
Serenading you in its tranquil song,
As it passes the rainbow and beyond the trees,
Singing in tune with the whispering leaves,
In that world of peace for you and I.

Salli Noble

A Musical Reflection

Relaxing is a luxury
Don't often get the chance
But when I do my thoughts stray on
My mind's eye to enhance.

I seem to hear the mighty sound
Of music from the 'Prom's
When all our hearts are lifted
By singers and their songs.

We sing of hope and glory,
From 'pomp and circumstance'
With Elgar's stirring music
We wave our flags and dance.

We feel that we are comrades all
Inspired to sway together
With joyfulness and rapture
And never mind the weather.

The people cheer, conductor smiles,
He wipes his brow and waits,
His is the power to 'raise the roof'
To Heaven's golden gates.

Why can't we be united so
At home, at work, at play
Good neighbours to our fellow men
So peace will come to stay?

Enid Hewitt

UNTITLED

A warm, sunny day
Perfect in every way
But you are not here
So it loses its appeal
Suddenly
The sun
Loses its brightness
The beach
The sea
Blurs from sight
You are not here
And I feel so sad
You cannot share
The good day we had
You cannot run on the beach
You can't paddle
In the sea
I smile at them
And hope they don't see
The sadness I feel
Or the pain they have come to know
I want them to be happy
I want them to feel alive
You have gone
Things change
We learn to cope
With everyday life
But it doesn't feel right
That you can't share
The sand between your toes
The warm sun on your face

Instead you are
Cold
Freezing cold
And lonely
And today
It is just not fair.

Debbie Alexander

KEEPIN' UP!

Drunk in charge
Of a stir fry
Bits get under
The plate.
Trying to keep
Some composure
In time with the evenin'
Date
Mushrooms slide out of the
Chopsticks
Sprouts over the lap
Regal prawns swim about
The rest is in a flap.
The good old days
Behind us -
Buns in front of the fire
Or best of all
On a Saturday night
Hot chips
From the ol'
Fish fryer!

Lyn Sandford

I Believe In Aliens

I believe in aliens
In case you didn't know
Roaming round the Earth
Those amazing UFOs.

Those wonderful crop-circles
Made from way up high
It's probably aliens having fun and games
In the dark night sky.

I wonder how they live?
I wonder how they dress?
I wonder if they have myths
Like Nessy in Loch Ness?

I bet they are looking down on us
From a planet, in a place
Oh yes, I know where they're looking from
They are looking from outside space

I bet they're either green or blue
Or maybe even yellow
'We're not either of those colours'
I bet they probably bellow.

Scientists have probably declared
'Aliens are not real'
But I bet, oh I'm sure I bet
That's not how they really feel.

They live in the third dimension
And do everything we dream
Think of all the things they can do
Like swimming in ice cream.

Do you believe aliens exist?
Think about it with concentration
All you really need to have
Is a bit of imagination!

Emily Jenkinson (10)

Boo!

In the dark, dark woods,
On a dark, dark night,
There was a cold, cold breeze,
And a cold, cold me.

The woods was spooky,
With shadows lurking everywhere.
The trees were swaying,
The bushes were rustling.

Eyes were peeping,
All looking for me,
From every branch,
On the tallest tree in the woods.

Then suddenly I heard footsteps
Getting louder and louder,
I turned around,
Then suddenly . . .

Boo!

Katie Ambroziak (10)

First Day At School

Shoes are polished, blouse is pressed,
Is it time? Is it time?
Rushed downstairs to get dressed,
Is it time - it must be time.
Porridge for breakfast -
Though I've hardly time to eat,
Holding tight to mother's hand,
I'm skipping down the street.
Then I see it - damp and mangled
Beside the pavement where I tread,
Draggled fur and limbs all tangled,
Lying in a pool of red.
Towards us runs a grey haired woman,
Scarlet apron, hair awry,
Clasps the messy, jumbled scrap
And to my horror starts to cry.
The crystal, sparkling day is shattered,
All thoughts of school have flown away,
'Mummy, Mummy, take me home,
I don't want to go to school today.'

Mary Daulton

THE SEA

Your voice is haunting as your great waves crash onto the sandy beaches.
Beneath your foaming surface a whole new world awaits.
The sand between my toes is comforting.
I dip my body under to discover the open doorway of your world.
Only to be shocked by the extent of our destruction.

Slowly emptying barrels pour out jet-black oil.
A cloud of it approaches me. I gasp for air and your black salty substance fills my lungs. The oil is coating the inside of my throat. As I take one last look at your peril and see the dead inhabitants of you, I make one last attempt to reach the surface before slowly floating to reach the murky depths of yourself where I shall lie for eternity in my watery grave.

Yet I must thank the sea for giving me such a vision of how it is being devastatingly destroyed, as this was the last realisation of the cruelties of man and our need to struggle to save it, before I died in the arms of the sea.

Your voice shall roar no more.

Jane Tomlin

WANT TO BUILD BRIDGES - NOT WALLS

I don't know when I started 'tho I know I was a babe in arms,
Sometime then I started building when experience set off my alarms.
Someone took away my mother's breast and I could no longer
                                                  hear her heart,
Lost the look of love she had, the bricks were gathering for me to start.
I no longer listened for a heart which I used to hear when cuddled tight,
A second mother reinforced my sentiments that cuddling just
                                                  wasn't right.
When I was reaching three foot tall my wall was much the same,
I didn't know what I was building, only knew it stopped the pain.
Time had set the mortar 'tho there's naught to see,
None can see but all can sense it, something in-between is shielding me.
'Tis sad for now I don't need it, but alas 'tis built to last,
The invisible wall is such a barrier which is built upon my past.
I'm searching for that someone who knows all about hidden walls,
They can teach me how to dismantle to make sure my barrier falls.
What was built for my protection now holds me like a vice,
I cannot break thru' my boundary and am seeking some advice.
                                                              Dear Lord . . .

Rosie Hues

THE KITE

Wizard ascends, trapezing the sky,
pulls and buffets to the whim of a clown
whose ringmaster on Earth does try
to hold the centre. Meanwhile, a kestrel hovers
but the kite resigns to tumble down.
Eternity or drown.

Spiralling wonder the acrobat flies
with such autonomy. The blue dome yawns
yet his reach denied by gravity, tries
to steal on the wind-whipped talons of light.
This blinds, amazes all those who stare.
Eternity, somewhere.

Waves, hammer and forge the cliffs from below,
while the sun warms the air and the thermals
rise, juggling maestro on a tightrope tow
to destiny. The child who binds the cords
restrains his dreams, defines his world.
Eternity is Now.

Adrian Mason

BUTTERFLIES IN THE BLACK FOREST

We walked beneath the vaulted pines
Awe-struck by a world of beauty,
Like columns in some great cathedral,
Soared the mighty trees.
And through the canopy above, sunbeams slanted,
Lighting the bushes on either side, catching the myriad spider webs,
All filigree and decked with sparkling diamond dew.
All this was ours, no sound or sight of other human life.
Hand in hand we walked and Time there had no meaning.
Then suddenly an alpine clearing, overhead a sky of brilliant blue.
And before our dazzled eyes a little meadow, flower-filled,
A joy of rainbow colours amid the waving grass
And everywhere the butterflies, blue butterflies dancing, dancing.
We stood entranced, speechless before such beauty,
You held me close and whispered, 'This we will always remember.'
In after-years, those dew-decked webs and butterflies
Kept our hearts close-bound throughout life's darker roads.
Though now I walk alone, I still remember
And in my heart our butterflies still dance.

G Hammler

LOVE'S EYE

Do not love me for my outward view
nor for my wealth or youth
look closely into my eyes there you will find the truth
for my eyes they cannot lie to show my heart's desire
that turns and churns inside of me
just like a ball of fire

Robin Morgan

A Poacher's Tale

In Lincolnshire woodland one winter's night,
the moon was full, the frost did bite.
With an old cock pheasant in the sight of my gun,
I'd a family to feed, with a new baby son.
Then from a distance I heard a cry
that echoed round that winter's sky.
A sound that seemed to stir the dead
and raise dark fears within my head.
Through the woods I started to run,
pheasant in hand and poacher's gun.
With moonlight shining through the trees,
and branches pointing eerily
to ghostly shadows dancing on the floor,
like phantoms from the world below.
I heard the cry call out once more -
much nearer than it was before,
through briars and bracken I seemed to fly
like a gust of wind that rushes by.
I raced in panic through mulch and mud,
'til at last I came to the edge of the wood.
Across the field and into the lane,
all my endeavours seemed in vain.
There I stood to regain my breath,
panting, sweating, scared to death.
Then once again the sound that chilled the night,
I turned and saw a wondrous sight -
two hares engrossed in a primeval dance,
crying, screaming, as if in a trance.
Then all my fears seemed to melt away,
as threatening darkness became light of day.

W J Oliver

THE WIND TURBINES OF MY MIND

A glance from my bedroom window filled me with utter dismay,
Anger welled into my brain cells, it was no ordinary day.
The panoramic view which met my gaze sounded an alarm,
For instead of the rolling pastures, there had sprouted a vast wind farm.

As far as my eyes could see there were triple Quixotic sails,
We're told they will be back up when fossil fuel fails.
To satiate our ever increasing electrical needs,
Instead of mere meaningless words, we now had hideous deeds.

'Generating for future generations', the politicians say
To safeguard for the future those living now must pay
With an eyesore across the landscape, for it's more than just a blot.
But the number of these monsters suggests Planning has lost the plot.

The droning in the wind caused by the sails monstrous twirling
Appeared as advancing hordes of dervishes a-whirling.
Speechless I may be but my thoughts are most elusive
For gigantic wind turbines make even power stations less intrusive.

As I survey the scene from the edge of Burton Height
I mourn the loss of the horizon, no longer within my sight.
York Minster no longer visible, even on the clearest of days,
And the wind farm has supplanted all else within my gaze.

But wait, I have just awoken, and to the window I run,
The sight delights my vision for of turbines there are none!
The open rolling landscape still remains supreme
And my worst fears are no more than a disturbing, subconscious dream.

John W Skepper

A Tonic From Our Father

Recently, while ill in bed,
Not even able to raise my head,
I laid on my side, and stared instead
At the view from my bedroom window.

I could only see the top half of the trees,
But I really couldn't have been more pleased
For as the day had just begun,
The birds were already feeding their young.

Flying to and from their nests until
Each baby bird had had its fill,
Time for a bath, they seem to think,
And flew down for a bath and a well earned drink.

Then once more I could see them at the top of the trees,
Preening themselves in the sun, and gentle breeze.
A few moments later, they all flew away,
For two baby squirrels had arrived to play.

Chasing each other around and around,
I thought, *any minute they'll fall to the ground,*
But they chased each other through the leaves,
And jumped from branch to branch with such expertise.

And then all of a sudden, as quick as they came,
They ran off, and the birds came back again.

I thank You Father, for this wonderful view,
A real 'tonic' it seems, to me from You.
We know Father, You work in mysterious ways,
I suddenly feel better than I have done for days.

Father, help us all to enjoy life's view,
And be grateful for all the blessings
We receive from You.

Marina Pugh

On The Shelf (Again)

I'm on the shelf (again)
With the peas and ham
And strawberry jam
After all these years of loving you!
I thought it was love -
But it wasn't true -
You found love through another's door
Get out, get out!
Now you can never be homeward bound
And I'm left on the shelf (again)
With the peas and ham -
And strawberry jam
Waiting for my boat to come ashore
Get out, get out!
As you go through someone else's door

Norma Spillett

Drawn

The wooden door propped open wide,
paintings beckoning 'come',
fat tubes of paint and turpentine
glisten in summer's sun.

Between the prints of Africa
find mists of Scottish glens.
Brushes of softest sable
compete with drawing pens.

The frames reflect my upturned face
seeking the artist's muse.
I move through reams of colour
to meet the one I choose.

Vivien Steels

DAILY REFLECTIONS

I love to hear the music,
Listen to Karen sing,
'I'm at the Top of the World',
Love's a wonderful thing.

I love, when other people,
Take pride in their work,
Pretty, kind and caring,
Diana didn't shirk.

I don't always understand,
What is on the telly,
Was there something underhand,
With the life of Dr Kelly?

These are people whom we've lost,
But we just carry on,
Please can we put our heads together,
Before someone else has gone.

Josie Pepper

Stranger On The Shore

I am a stranger on your shore,
brought to you on a sea of tranquillity,
blessed, to be yours for evermore
to share a life of love to infinity.

Hand in hand we will stroll on in the sands of time,
our footprints for evermore washed by quiet waters
to disappear only momentarily in a lifetime
then once more appearing with love in quiet backwaters.

Our love's serenity will be in the stars at night,
would this stranger who upon your shore did stand
have known that he would find love's sprite,
to hold within his heart this, your wonderland.

John Clarke

Frozen

We face windward,
Close our eyes,
Let providence embrace us in spectral arms,
As gusts carry our prayers
Across a glacial world.

Finally they come to rest,
Billions of hopes frayed and frozen,
Stilled and silent,
Creating a vast, cold tundra
Of lifeless wishes,
Fields of ice
That touch our hearts.

Edwin Page

ANCIENT OAK

Astride the nook where branch and trunk embrace,
a fleet of children sailed to pilgrim shores
and lovers lingered in your shade, to trace
the paths which laced two parted lives once more.

Drawn by moon's glow, a cloud of moths arose,
as if your bark erupted into flight,
and dawn brought colonies of greys, who stole
fat acorns to sustain their winter nights.

A road now binds your roots, cements your soil,
and life is trapped within the speeding lights.
Exhaust fumes make the stifled air taste stale.

To toast the route of progress, old trees fall
as space is cleared for climbing frames and slides,
where children play in line behind the rails.

Jan Harris

LATE NIGHT BREAK

The warmth of the evening fire
Flickering orange and yellow tongues beneath the hearth
The primitive in the modern setting.
Outside the glow of midnight stars
Sparkling frost on winter pavements
Serenading the dreams of a thousand sleepers
Setting in rhythms on the cold glass
The orange glow of a cut glass tumbler
Of single malt
Catching the lights in the Christmas tree
And just for a moment
I find perfect peace.

M J Gray

PAST TIME

Sitting in a p***-stained chair, unaware
bones withered, not as sturdy as tree twigs
reviewing mind freight from the past days
his essence, these alien structures with doublespeak seldom known.

A half body, crumpled, paper-like ball
dainty as the petals of a bereaved rose,
yet twisted crude metal, colder now than before
flowers ruffle in the cool evening air.

Long time ago, a fighter, a drinker,
a father, on occasion a lover and a frequent thinker
he once made honey love beneath a wispy willow tree
now a nurse wipes his haunches at eleven and three.

Bellows by mere children, we fought to save all,
this champion from bygone, the poke and provoke,
this adrift generation wait for clock time to kick into view
this downtrodden soldier, recalls when he was the man who . . .

Luke Kayne

SALVATION

In desperate shape screaming a voiceless name
I lie limp in need of a tourniquet
But one won't come along today

Praying you'll be the perfect fit
You look like you will,
But you can't stem the tide of the predator's kill.

Caroline Roe

NOTHING BUT...

Glistening eyes I see before me
A calming look of ease
Nothing but a look from you
Can bring me to my knees.

A gentle whisper into my ear
A warm kiss upon my cheek
Nothing but a touch from you
Makes me feel so weak.

I am shivering with anticipation
Wishing you would pull me near
Nothing like making love to you
Makes it all so clear.

I will want you for all days to come
I will feel love for you always, it's true
However wrong it is to some
I just can't live my life without you.

Danielle Watts

WHAT'S IN A MARRIAGE?

    a *m*erging of two people in love
      *a*cceptance - appreciation - adoration
A bit of *r*ough and tumble, is always fun!
  While *r*eal life and reason still abounds!
     *i*ndividuality still remains - with acceptance of
                        each other's ways.
    *a*greeing to compromise, when necessary
  The *g*ood relationship continues to grow
    *e*merging in every lasting enlightenment and
                   continued friendship.

Cheryl Campbell

A Lincolnshire Yellow Belly

Born and bred in Lincolnshire, what a marvellous place to be
If you have never been to Lincolnshire, then you have a lot to see
You will never see a better scene than on a summer's day in June
Everything looks so beautiful and the birds are in full tune

The greatest cathedral in England stands proudly on the hill
A short ride across to Boston, the Stump another thrill
Just up the road at Conningsby is the Battle of Britain Flight
Across the fens you could see the Red Arrows, now that will be a sight

A day at Woodhall Spa, see the Dam Busters' monument shining
                                                            brightly in the square
Or motor through the Wolds and breathe in some nice sea air
There's Skegness, Mablethorpe, Cleethorpes, Sutton on Sea
All lovely places to spend a day, many things to see

Our historic monuments are scattered right across the shire
There's Old Bollingbrook Castle where old Cromwell battled there
Tattersall Castle you can see from many miles away
The castle up the hill in Lincoln would take another day

You must bring your friends to Lincolnshire and show them everything
There's something here for everyone, whatever friends you bring
I am proud to be a yellow belly, what a marvellous place to be
When you have had a taste of Lincolnshire, there'll be more
                                                            you want to see

Len Woodhead

HEAVEN

Whither shall my jocund feet pass?
Echo: Grass.

On springy green of dewy lawn:
Echo: Dawn.

Where golden sun spreads hope and light:
Echo: Sight.

Horizon mists make cloudy air:
Echo: Prayer.

Sweet chorus of the morning hymn:
Echo: Him.

Brings strange joy to heart and ears:
Echo: Tears.

Scented paths before me lie:
Echo: Sigh.

To heal, restore and kindly show:
Echo: Know.

I'll walk alone my hand in His:
Echo: Bliss.

Helen Drewett

AUTUMN'S STRATEGY

Autumn has crept on us almost unawares
As we dallied by the stream, watching fish glide
Through warm, gold rills from one cool, shady nook
To another, deeper, darker, colder.

Autumn has come slowly, sliding into place
As we watched the raindrops glisten on the petals,
Heard the lazy murmur of busy bees
Ravishing the generous flowers of summer.

Autumn has come quietly, stealing through the woods
As we formed field daisies into necklaces,
And lay there idly dreaming in long grass
Rippling around us in the summer breeze.

Now autumn is upon us, startled we see
The bending grass is turning sere and brown, the leaves
Are drying up, the corn is cut and stored,
The harvest soon be gathered in once more.

We struggle, we protest the hardening grip,
Trying to turn back to days of warmth and languor,
But in the end we will accept this change,
Sweet harbinger of cosy Christmas cheer.

Margaret Pagdin

BELL, BOOK AND CANDLE

The flame flickered wildly, the air grew quite thick
I knew they were near. My stomach felt sick
I heard the bell toll and I knew it was time
I had waited so long. I had followed the sign.

I knew the rules well. I had read all the books
I had given my life yet still more they took
Again I still waited, but all was in vain
The tension had mounted 'til I was in pain

I crouched in the corner. I made myself small
I could hear hushed whispers outside in the hall
I held my breath close, no noise did I utter
The trembling grew worse. My heart now a'flutter

Again the bell tolled and I felt myself sway
The voices grew closer. I started to pray
The door opened slowly but I stood firm my ground
As the creatures then entered, my sanctuary found

They stood there before me and I was struck dumb
And then came the question, 'Is it teatime yet, Mum?'

Jennifer Davey

Laughter And Tears

Don't cry with tears of sorrow
Cry with tears of jubilation,
For every moment of sadness
There's one of exhilaration.
For everyone that leaves this world . . .
Their day now finally done,
A newborn child is sent to us,
Their life still yet to run.
Every day that God sends
Is a day of 'ying' and 'yang',
For everyone whoever cried
There are two birds that sang.
Evening comes to every day
And darkness fills the sky,
Then the dawn comes creeping
And soon the sun's on high.
Without sadness in our lives
We would not see the glee,
All things need a contrast
This is laughter and tears to me.

Judi Whitehouse

BEING

Everyday nonsense is making me dizzy
I'm lying on a mattress surveying the sky
The world is revolving and everyone's busy
I'm static like stalagmite, not caring why
This is me time - be time
Time to wallow and wander
To dream and believe, imagine and ponder
Get lost in a maze
Alone in your daze
Marooned in a trance as your mind starts to dance
And the minor chord is magic even though it makes you cry
And the major seventh heavenly - you sit back and sigh
Let the little babies sleep
There is no need to weep
Just be happy you are living and breathing and
Seeing and hearing and feeling
The beat of your heart.

W E Deweltz

UNTITLED

Running
Late for his train
Takes out his pocket watch
Time in hand; he's late. Time is not
In hand.

Janet Erskine

BABBLING BROOK

While strolling by a babbling brook
I took the time to take a look
To see the trout make its run
In full view of the morning sun

Then soon a dragonfly passes by
It lands on reeds and rests awhile
Then off again with wings that gleam
Across the little babbling stream

Over the water nymph flies land
The old brown trout he thinks it's grand
A splash of water you will hear
Another meal for you my dear

Now time has come for me to go
I took a look and there I know
That life goes on from day to day
In the sun while we work and play.

Ronald Claxton

FADE YOU MY LOVE THIS NIGHT

Fade you my love this night,
The moon grows ever pale,
Would ne'er a heart as quite,
Fade you my love this night,
And ever seems so bright,
Or eyes, so never fail,
Fade you my love this night,
The moon grows ever pale.

Christopher W Wolfe

A Summer Day Of Discoveries

Somewhere interesting and somewhere new,
An escape, a challenge always beckons you.
When joining trippers on a coach for a day,
Relaxing as the city fades, joyfully we speed away.

The peaceful countryside soon comes into view,
Hills and dales, towns and pretty villages too.
Bakewell by name, known for its delicious pies,
Shops, pubs round a market, with many a surprise.

From May to September Well Dressings are found,
'Water worship' started by Celts, in Derbyshire all around.
A wooden board soaked, adding clay, berries, leaves and flowers,
Beautiful, religious pictures are transformed, taking many hours.

These large Well Dressings are hidden everywhere,
Often difficult discovering them, but must not despair.
Meeting others walking, discovering some in the park,
One made by the Scouts, a white dog, visible in the dark.

Climbing a hill, around a corner, standing by a church gate,
A beautiful, colourful scripture scene, amazingly did relate.
Each one a masterpiece, when eventually, joyfully discovered,
Yes, the rain came, and by umbrellas we were all covered.

In 1349 Tissington in Derbyshire revised this annual art,
There are many villages, and nearly everyone plays a part.
Heavenly water is vital for every living thing,
Yearly Derbyshire continues, with their special thanksgiving.

Stella Bush-Payne

The Song Of The Fly
(A poem in quatrains)

A defenceless little housefly, oh look!
Swat quickly with this newspaper or book,
But saw with my hundred efficient eyes,
And dodged the swipe with the 'take-off' I took.

When in-flight I can roll, loop or a bunt,
And wonder who else can do such a stunt,
I can land on ceiling and walk down glass;
So much given me; such a tiny runt.

I have many relatives, large and small,
Some have nasty stings, bites and wings have all,
A very small one - big problem for man,
I look for webs, birds and spiders on the wall.

My nephews like to fly o'er waters still,
To dabble their hot feet and drink their fill,
I told them it's such a dangerous thing,
One day, splash, and one returned not, ne'er will.

One of our kind hunts over every rill,
Has double wings and glides with ease at will,
Lovely shape, an iridescent body,
Catches and eats my kith and kin with skill.

Met the love of my heart the other day,
We flew and danced around with naught to say,
With each other we rubbed our wings - and kissed,
On some scrap meat, what lovely eggs she lay.

A host of good children we did not lack,
Who changed to copies of ourselves - a knack.
What a lovely family to behold,
What an active swarm to fly there and back.

My love flew one night into a dark cave,
From such a eerie place, the thrill it gave,
A very quiet 'whoosh' was all I heard,
No cry for help, from a spot like a grave.

Oh the pain, the grief that now smothers me,
Without you, my true love, never to see,
But, this Heaven where man says all will meet,
Will there be room for little flies to be?

Edward E Gregory

A Friend Is . . .

A friend is someone who is always there,
To listen to your problems that you need to share.
A friend is someone in which you can confide,
You can be yourself, there's no need to hide.
A friend is someone on which you can rely,
Share your happiness or the tears when you cry.
A friend is someone that will never judge,
Never cause you harm or hold a grudge.
A friend is someone with which you can relate,
Be glad that you met and feel it is fate.
A friend is someone that will never turn you away,
Whether you need them night or day.
A friend's actions show they care,
This special bond is precious and rare.
A friend will be there through and through,
I'm so lucky because my friend is you.

Tania M Taylor

Nostalgia

Bakelite radios tuned to radio four
Rediffusion wired, no electricity at all
Fragile gas mantles dotted around the room
A black grated hearth keeping us warm.

Outside toilet in a shared backyard
Large black dog tethered and keeping guard
Newspaper squares hanging on string
A line stretched taught for Monday's washing.

Trolley buses, trams, steam trains as well,
Coke and coal fires, log burning smell
Beano and Dandy, Bunty, Girls' Friend
Pocket money for sweets at the weekend.

Childhood games of skipping and ball
Hoola hoops, hopscotch, leapfrog and all
No wasted minutes, no idle time
No vandals or muggers or street crime.

Money was tight and well spent
Dinners, clothing, bus fare and rent
Each moment counted, every day
School, homework, work or play.

Childhood memories happy and sad
Of times long gone when you were a lad
It's not like that now, you were telling your son
Progress changed it for everyone.

Jacqui Beddow

THE BALLAD OF THE BURNT OUT CLUTCH

I once set out for the Stretton hills
On an ancient bike and chair*,
With a wife and babe, two teenage girls,
A kitten (or a pup) and lots of sup,
For a day in the clean, fresh air.

Returning over Wenlock Edge
A thunderstorm we saw.
It was not too near so we had no fear.
The lightning struck like an angry buck
And we heard the thunder roar.

We made our way to Wenlock town
But on the Bridgnorth road,
The clutch burnt out, the storm caught up,
The street lamps failed, the rain came down
And the wind just blowed and blowed.

We moved into a B & B
And dried our soggy gear,
With a wife and babe, two teenage girls,
A kitten (or a pup) but very little sup.
In the morning, the sky was clear.

I took the bus to Wellington
Through a most enchanting view,
The Ironbridge Gorge, the ancient bridge;
I got the parts and fixed the bike,
Then we knew what we must do.

We sold our house in Birmingham
And moved out Ironbridge way,
And many the years, some dressed with tears,
Have passed between the changing scene
But we're still there to this day.

*sidecar

John Belcher

BALLAD

A maiden sings as she spins the thread
To weave the sheets for her marriage bed;
Her sometime lover sailed away,
Vowing he would return one day,
But as the maiden tired of waiting
Half her loving turned to hating;
Now she spins forever faster,
In the shadow of disaster.

She sings about the mystic table
Known in ancient myth and fable:
'Life and death, love and hate,
Opposites are separate;
Light and darkness, good and evil,
Sun and moon, male and female,
True and false, false and true,
You and I, I and you.'

As she chants her poor thoughts wander,
Absence makes the heart grow fonder,
But when absence is protracted
Woman's heart becomes distracted;
Now I fear her mind is smitten,
Like a plant diseased and bitten,
Like an ash tree after lightning,
All its countenance is frightening;

Grey and leafless, gaunt and cold,
Or like an oak tree, gnarled and old;
Her looks have withered since his leaving,
Nothing can allay her grieving:
'I and you, you and I,
You shall live and I shall die,'
She cries, and spins forever faster,
In the shadow of disaster.

Dorothy Buyers

TRAFFIC LIVES

Cocooned in my shell, waiting in the traffic
My daily bungee jump to work

I see the woman in her world
A red Nova. She sings.
Opening and closing her mouth
An empty mime to watchers on

A blue Rover. A man on the phone
Intent, picking invisible lint off his carefully selected sweater

A new Beetle
A strange, spotty youth caged safely within
Both mind and motor in neutral
Picking his nose then trailing his fingernail on his bottom lip

Nice

I look right

A woman with loss in her eyes. Ordinary in every way
Showing years beyond her youth. She looks lost and uneasy
An unfamiliar face shares my journey
Each morning I see her

She vacantly returns my gaze
Shades of grey, she never smiles

One day in the rain
I saw her crying
While the world washed over her
Head in her hands

An age of empty hopes consumes
She is my reflection

Shirley Cawte

ANOTHER REALM

As I perform my morning rites
Of exercise, a tardy fox
Is combing lawn for final snack
Before retiring for the day.
We cox and box, as he must wake
When I decide it's time for bed.
As creature cursed by need to hunt
By night, no drop of pity dwells
Within his eyes. Without a twinge
Of guilt he gulps a clutch of eggs
A thrush has just begun to brood.
By day I relish colours on
Display. But when they start to fade
It's time for fox to prowl again.
But since the moon is up a sheen
Of gentle light ignites each leaf
And silent pond. So I delay
My time for rest and wander free
Beneath the stars with thankful heart
At thought of wife and friends. Our days
On earth are brief indeed but griefs
Cannot expunge the joys received
Before our final curtains fall
And we explore another realm.
Are those who choose to dwell in dark
Just beasts who fear and shun the light?
Or will they too have gained reprieve
When love's embrace is felt at last?
Despite his cruel ways, I feel
A stealthy welcome for my fox.

Henry Disney

WHEN YOU'RE NOT THERE

I wait 'til you're all gone, to cry out my heart,
I wait 'til you're all gone, to cut myself apart;
You see the aftermath and start to cry,
Those tears for my blood make me want to die.
This pain is for me; can't you just close your eyes?
Pretend this isn't happening; ignore the screams and lies.
Blood-stained bandages thrown away into the bin,
One cut and scar, for every lie and sin.
Blood and tears absorbed in tissues, when you're not there,
I do it when you're not around, because I don't want you to care.
This isn't happening; I'll lie until you believe me,
These cuts and burns, I don't want you to see.
Suicide notes, prepared for 'the worst',
All this is in my head, I'm ready to burst,
I want it gone; I know you want it gone too,
But I'll keep it to myself; can't you see I'm protecting you?

Sarah Sproston

THIS WORLD

We are born into this world innocent and free
Forever pursuing destiny
Searching for happiness and needing to be seen
To fit into life's big scheme

In a society of lost souls and a world full of woe
Forever searching for a direction to
In the hope that one day we will find
The recognition and love that beholds mankind

Korena Marie Baker

LIFE AND LOVE

What is life all about
I have no clue without a doubt
But we muddle through as best we can
In hope we find the master plan

We fall in love now and again
But when it ends there's such great pain
Somehow though we still try
To find ourselves another gal or guy

The soul is willing
We go on living
The heart may ache
But the chance we'll take

You see the souls we have
Deep down are built brave
They will carry us far if we let them
Through life, and love and things we can't fathom

When we were young we wanted to grow
If only we knew then what we now know
Enjoyed the youth, no cares just fun
Friends aplenty, no worrying to be done

Then come the teenage years
Bringing parents many fears
The first date, that first kiss
The changing body, the bullying I will not miss

Then before you know it you're an adult
How did that happen? Body fills out, what an insult
Life is slipping away, before your eyes
Running quickly, no time to try and work out the whys

Quick it's going, without you knowing
Don't sit down and stop, what you doing?
There's always something around that corner
You may have to fight that little bit harder

But this is life and we are not here long
Do your best and remain strong
Life is a precious gift that not all get
So pick yourself up and stop the regret

Life is what you make it
Love is there to help you through it
When times get tough call your friends
They will help you take the right bends

You may feel different, I don't know
Just my feelings I wanted to show
Love life, friends and family
After all they are the ones who make you smiley

Sarah Clark

SALLY BROWN

Young Sally Brown
Went for a swim but thought she might drown.
And so with a frown
She reached for her gown,
Thinking she might as well go back to town.
Being hungry and thirsty she popped into The Crown
Went to a table and then she sat down.

Zoe French

Been Done Before

Been done before
through the crack
in the marriage
in the flung wide door;

Out flies a temper,
cooling:
remembers it dissembles
to be wiped by the floor.

Returning cold to colder
through a more
contrite gap
in the never settled score.

Peter Asher

One Rule

One rule for you, another for me,
One rule for the captive, one rule for the free.
One rule based on history, one rule based on lies,
You rule over me, no one hears my cries.

One rule grown from arrogance, one rule grown on fear,
One rule is high profile but one you'll not hear.
One rule for convenience, one rule for your gain,
Whilst you live in comfort, I'm dying in pain.

One rule for the sick, one rule for the well,
One rule formed in Heaven, one rule forged in Hell.
One rule for the captive, one rule for the free,
Yes . . . it's one rule for you, another for me.

Stuart Wood

LOVE'S BLACK TRUTH

I hear the whispers of passing dreams
They only pass me by
I drown in shallow water, I drown myself for you
Simple desires are lost
If you wanted me you could understand
These words would have meaning, they would awaken you
Are you awake now?
This is a dream, my dream, a dream of contentment,
An eternal dream
Of one I love, for all I know of you
I hate the pain you cause me,
I hate that you do not love me, that it is wasted on you
I cry and sting and bleed for this lost cause
I don't want to bleed anymore
Let this dig deep, hope is no longer my ally
I lost you long ago
Or even worse I never had you

Bryony Freeman

MALVERN HILLS

We can gaze from the hills
See the church, it looks so still
Winter greenness and drops of dew
Hung on the grass and bushes too
There's a small sleeping town
Through a wood and open ground
Our paths are clear but grass is dry
The sun turns gold in the sky

Ann Thompson

A Hill In Korea

We had been sent to the hill with orders to hold,
It's very important is what we were told,
The enemy commander must have had the same thought,
You can tell by the way that his men have fought.

All day long they have pressed their attack,
All day long we have driven them back.
Their dead are piled high in front of our lines,
Some killed by our bullets, and some by our mines.

We've suffered casualties too in this 'bloody' fight,
Our dead comrades lie to our left and our right,
Let's hope that they have not given their lives in vain,
And that they will be remembered when peace comes again.

There is young Tommy who never meant anyone harm,
He was happy working on his father's farm,
But the army called for him, and sent him to war,
Now he won't be driving his plough anymore.

There's Ken from London, always one with a joke,
He came from nice, down to earth folk,
He was proud to have been born within the sounds of Big Ben,
Now he will never hear them chiming again.

And then there was Gerry, he was such a great guy,
He was always a comfort when danger was nigh,
There were some others including Jimmy and Don,
A mortar blast meant that they had all gone.

We've lost some good men, and no doubt we'll lose more,
Before we have finished with this terrible war,
One day it will end but only God knows when,
There's more shooting and shouting they are coming again.

Once more we have managed to repel the attack,
Once more we have managed to drive the enemy back,
This time we've lost Cyril, Freddy and Bill
What a terrible price we have paid for this hill.

Ron Martin

MOTHER

Mothers are like diamonds
A girl's best friend
Always there when you need them
A helping hand to lend
Her shoulder is a cushion
For tears that you may cry
Always knowing the answers
To the questions you ask, why?
Never interfering
When you need to be alone
A hot dinner, a cup of tea
Waiting when you come home

So make sure that you tell your mom
How much you love her so
It's often an easy mistake to make
But she doesn't always know.

Ruth Fellows

FAIRIES

Magical world,
toadstool houses,
peering out,
little eyes,
hearing laughter,
twinkly lights,
colours array.
Magical world,
fun for everyone,
food eaten,
games played,
tiny quilts,
where they lay,
during the day,
awake at night,
where they may fly,
sparkly wings.
Magical world
living with wildlife,
all shapes and sizes,
close your eyes,
see if you can see a fairy.

Emma Jane Lambert

A Forest Scene

Morning sun filters through forest trees,
Shafts of light setting mystic scenes.
Sounds of nature, woodpecker tapping,
A pigeon's wings flapping, clapping.

In the stillness of an autumn day,
This stage is set, with a sun's ray.
The darkness of the forest like night,
Yet here is a beam of light so bright.

Yes! A mystic stage of nature true,
Above the sky, cloudless blue.
Leaves changing, from green to gold,
Shimmering, falling onto the earthy mould.

A robin twitters, marking its patch,
A squirrel, the earth, its little paws scratch,
Its nuts will store, before winter's bite,
Its larder buried, well out of sight.

The shadows long as the days grow short,
Each day the scene a different sort,
Still hear that woodpecker, above tapping,
Or that pigeon, its wings flapping, clapping . . .

Alan J Morgan

FRIENDSHIP

Love comes and it goes, joy comes and it goes,
The seesaw of life never ends
But whoever you are and wherever you are
The best part of life is your friends.

They are there thro' the thick, they are there thro' the thin,
They are there with a smile and a wink,
They are there thro' the ups, they are there thro' the downs,
They are there when you sometimes can't think.

The sorrows and losses of life's turning tides,
When death and despair have no ends
The reason for doing, for enduring the loss
Is possible - due to your friends.

The family are there giving joy and despair,
Giving hope, giving birth, giving strife.
But my future is often helped on its way
By the friends I have made in my life.

It works in reverse, you give of yourself,
When a friend is in need, or in pain.
To someone so special they make life worthwhile
To your friends - again and again.

My life has not always been as it should
The path that I chose had its bends,
But I have made it through all the gates and the turns
Due to my wonderful, faithful friends.

Ayleen Brown

I Know

I know, I know just what you cannot tell,
I know and understand so well,
And yet your silent heart is heard,
You need not say a single word,
I know and understand.

I think I know what you would say,
Words I have longed to hear for many a day,
But I know that you feel constrained,
And because of your silence your heart is pained,
I know this and I understand.

But if you would make my heart rejoice,
You have no need to use your voice,
Simply look into my eyes and if it's true what I believe,
And if my eyes do not deceive,
Then simply hold my hand,
And I will know and understand.

Ron Martin

Music

There's nothing quite like music to give your heart a glow,
It lifts you up and floods your mind till it will overflow.

The velvet sound a cello makes, sits softly in your ears,
The violin so smooth and rich will bring forth silent tears.

The oboe and the clarinet, an aching, yearning sound,
And next to these the dulcet tones of flutes are to be found.

And finally the harpsichord with gorgeous flowing themes,
Will seize your heart and fill your head with quiet, lovely dreams.

Muriel Waldt

THE ZOMBIE

On a dark, dark night
From a dark, wet grave
There's hideous sight
Of which we're not saved

A foul stench rises
The coffin lid breaks
There are no prizes
For guessing what awakes

One eye only has this fiend
His skin is torn and rotting
The tongue hangs off, with teeth uncleaned
Strands of muscle knotting

He stumbles in his search for flesh
An arm breaks like a twig
So up again to start afresh
Moaning like a pig

At last he spies a well-lit house
He knows there's food inside
Humans, a dog, cat or mouse
All of which he's tried

The door opens, too quick for him
A crushing force is felt
He loses every major limb
His fatal blow is dealt

As his head rolled down the hill
The humans stepped outside
To this day they wonder still
What they hit that cried

Adam Poole

OUR GRANNY

When Granny Fisher came to stay
Our best behaviour was on display.
With her hair in a bun, with coal-black eyes,
Our immediate obedience was no surprise.

Peering at us through little round glasses,
We'd certainly not risk taking our chances!
Not shouting out, just using love,
No rod of iron, just a velvet glove.

With her black button shoes, wool stockings of grey
And her long dark skirts - Victorian to the day.
She wore a 'dickey' front fixed with a cameo,
Appearing covered up almost from head to toe.

(Eldest sister Jessie filled the other three sisters with shock
When she flew back here from Canada with permed hair
and a short, floral frock!)
Gran lived with our aunt for most of the year,
Whose house, in the next village, was really quite near.

Her bedding smelling of lavender, her clothing and even her skin,
This smell will always remind me of this lovely lady, our kin.
When things were lost, just couldn't be found, had gone
completely astray,
'They'll be up in Annie's room behind the clock,' the family
would all say.

'I laughed hearty', and 'Up timber hill to bed',
Were some of her sayings we often heard said.
Born in circa eighteen hundred and seventy-five
But the memories of our gran are still much alive.

E Marcia Higgins

FEAR

My heart is corrupted by darkness,
It races round to get out of this prison.
I am falling down deeply,
Silently, softly and calmly.
I fear the worst.
What will happen to my family?
What will happen to my friends?
What's happening to me?
I can see nothing but the dark.
Shadows coming towards me.
Slipping, sliding and creeping.
What are they doing to me?
I now see a light,
Small but visible.
Where is it from?
I know!
It's from my heart.
I must make the light stronger.
Think Damian think.
Of course, my family, my friends.
I think of my family,
Mum, Dad, Brother, Sister.
I think of my friends,
Everything they have done for me.
Stronger the light is, I still have my life,
Or is it my turn to go,
My turn to be someone,
My chance to take a risk?
The ground is visible.
I am ready,
For my big performance.

Damian Lomas (13)

LOVE IS A RENGA

Love is wonderful,
It's a tingle in the loins,
And fluttering heart.

Hungry pouting of the lips,
A tongue yearning to enter,

Hands that long to search around,
And see what secrets they find,

Bodies long to touch and join,
Limbs that yearn to intertwine,

Kisses sweeter than fine wine,
Bodies throbbing with passion,

A love-knot forms and is tied,
The ultimate expression.

The feeling is quite unique,
The most natural desire.

There is nothing in the world,
Like the act of making love.

Poets have waxed eloquent,
About the feeling of love.

Procreation depends on
The physical act of love.

Mick Nash

THE DEVIL MAY CARE

I felt the wings of an angel brush against my face,
So soft and gentle, and then, I was taken in an embrace,
I heard a voice then whisper, close up to my ear,
'The Lord has sent me down to Earth, with this message clear.'

He wants you to follow him, and preach his word today,
And he wants the people of the world to change their wicked way,'
I stood there transfixed by these words, wondering what to do,
When the Devil appeared on the scene, he had a message too

I asked the Devil and angel, what was in it for me?
The angel said my reward would be in Heaven, as I would surely see,
I told the Heavenly angel I could do with something now,
Money would make heaven on Earth, if he could arrange it somehow.

The angel said it could not be done, and that I would have to wait,
Until the day that I could die, on a later date,
The Devil was standing near, a smile upon his face,
He said, 'You come with me, I've got money in my place.'

I then asked the Devil, how long I would have to wait,
He then got out a cheque book, and wrote in the present date,
He then gave me the cheque and this is what he said,
'You can fill in the amount you want, don't wait until you're dead.'

I thought about the money and in my mind I began to count,
I held a pen within my hand and slowly wrote in the amount,
I then turned towards the angel, and this is what I said,
'Will you tell the Lord I prefer my money long before I'm dead?'

The angel then looked at me with a glint within his eye,
And said it looked as if I would have a good time long before I die,
I then spoke to the angel, 'Why don't you come with me
And we will spend the dough together? How happy we will be.'

The angel thought it over, and then said with a smile,
'I think I will come and stay with you, at least for a while,
And we will go and paint the town red, and have a lot of fun,
I'm going to leave the kingdom of God I'm going on the run.

And so we both went out that evening, partying on the town,
We had a lot of money, in fact ten million pound,
We both acted like devils, drinking for all our worth,
The angel said, 'Goodbye Heaven, I have more fun on Earth.'

And so he is still here drinking, and we both agree,
We have another drinking partner, the Devil he makes three,
And so we will go on drinking till the very end,
I've never seen the face of 'God', but the devil is my friend.

W J R Dunn

URBAN DEMISE

Crash! That's a car window gone.
Wires ripped out and steering column wrecked.
Where will it go? No one knows.
A sure fired destiny awaits its end,
There'll be no recognition.
Burnt out at some desolate ground.
There could be a glorified chase
Through the streets, going the wrong way,
Not a care or even aware.
Ending in a role, abandoned on some road
In a far away place.
Alarms ring out, is it for real or is it a fault?
No notice is taken anymore,
Just another annoying alarm.

Wendy Brittain

Addict

They view it all
Through hungry eyes
And can't disguise
Their future lies
In misery and despair

They see it all
Yet they are blind
Cannot escape the ties that bind
No explanation can they find
Of how fate put them there

They watch and see
Their lives slip by
And though they try
They can't deny
The desperate aching need

The others state
And wait their turn
They know the craving will return
They pray their loved ones will not learn
The habit that they feed

Ever downward they descend
Thieve from family and friend
Every penny they will spend
Until the need is met

Pointless though their lives may seem
Shambling blankly in a dream
Their soulless eyes, still clouded scream
Dear God, has death come yet

Sheila Jane Hobson

PATIENCE REQUIRED

Farmers in tractors
Sitting on high
Vehicles in convoy
Trying to pass by
Trundling along
At a leisurely pace
Patience required
Not a race
Farming implements
Towing wide
Flashing orange lights
On either side
Moving slowly
From field to field
Working year round
Crops to yield
Around country lanes
Not a moment to spare
Motorists still queuing
In total despair
Signal at last
Tractor turning right
Drivers accelerate
Clear road ahead
Not a tractor in sight.

Brenda M Hadley

IN MY TIME

I am growing old now, with a tale of war and misery
I am a living witness to this terror, in my memory
Nightmares haunt me still, like a camera my inner eye,
Gun fire, war planes raining bombs from the sky,
People killed with shrapnel,
Sharp like a sword from the shell.

One night in an air raid,
I saw the lace market ablaze,
The flames leap high, make the sky glow red,
They tend the wounded and count the many dead,
A community air raid shelter, took a direct hit,
They dig in the debris, for people buried in the pit.

There is the smell of acrid smoke,
As we run for cover, cough and choke,
Down in the shelter like a tomb,
Cold and damp with beetles, thoughts of doom,
We sincerely pray, 'Please let the enemy go away,'
The all-clear sounds at the break of day.

We stand and stare in shocked dismay,
Houses from across the road, are blown away,
By the kerb side at our feet,
Lay stretchers, silent, covered in sheet,
So still in the first light of the sun,
They have gone to Heaven everyone.

Seasons bring rain and snow,
In the ruins wildflowers in abundance grow,
Poppy, daisy, noonday, willow, herb,
Seeds scattered by wind and bird,
Frail flowers that persevere and grow through rock to bloom,
Give hope, a healing balm in this place of gloom.

V Sinclair

THE SECOND LEASE OF LIFE - *RETIREMENT*

Now working days are laid to rest
Relaxed pleasures are put to the test

The schedules and stresses of working life
Are behind us with far less strife

One can enjoy life at a leisurely pace
Deciding daily routine, and whom to face

Choosing *when* and *where* to go out
This is what freedom is all about

Senior moments may come to the fore
Which you laugh off, and others *ignore*

Time to observe wildlife in much detail
Feeding the birds every day without fail

Appreciating memories of our *happy times*
Forgetting the sad ones, now left behind

Grateful for good things life brought our way
And making the most of each *new* day.

Diana Joy Hawes

ARDEN IS GONE

Since late Middle Ages
Arden began steadily shrinking
From the demand
For fuel, timber for building,
More arable ploughland.

Though in the pages
Of plays, Shakespeare writes
Of Arden nostalgically
As a more secret, secluded place,
Its woods in his days
Had dwindled significantly
To mere remnants
Of their former vastness.

Now, Arden is gone;
Probably never again
Will strangers, distressed,
Lose their way in its fastness,
Or even its dwellers stray,
Find themselves alone,
Lost in the Forest.

David Daymond

AN ANTHEM TO A CHIP SHOP IN WINTER
(To the tune of 'God Save The Queen')

It's very cold tonight, good for the appetite, let's have some chips.
After a drink or two, only one thing to do, let's have some chips.
Protein and vitamins, who thinks about such things?
Forgive this least of sins,
let's have some chips.

Queuing out of the rain, icy winds blow in vain,
let's have some chips.
Warm, pungent atmosphere, smells that we all hold dear,
let's have some chips.
Hot pies and saveloys, fritters and curry sauce,
eat them without remorse, let's have some chips.

Bags full of solid gold, eat them before they're cold,
enjoy your chips.
Cod fillets golden brown, dispel the meanest frown,
have some more chips.
Haddock and mushy peas, wonderful antifreeze,
heaven by small degrees, what lovely chips.

Wander home wearily, chip filled and beerily, thank God for chips.
Care for your home and town, don't throw your litter down,
I just love chips.
Transport of pure delight, best food to eat at night,
relish it with all your might, enjoy your chips . . .

Chris L Robbs

SIDNEY SNAIL

Sidney Snail slipped quickly along,
With his house upon his back,
Well never had I seen a snail,
Move quite as fast as that.

Then I saw the reason why,
A song thrush sat in a tree,
He had got his beady eye on Sid,
He wanted Sid for tea.

He spread his wings, he floated down,
He landed at Sidney's side,
But Sid had slipped into his house,
And closed the door behind.

The song thrush picked up Sidney's house,
He hopped over to a stone,
And I heard the terrible crack and crash,
As he dismantled poor Sid's home.

He pulled Sid out of the rubble,
With his very pointed beak,
He opened it wide, Sid slipped inside,
And I heard his mournful shriek.

These mournful words I heard Sid cry,
As he slipped down that thrush's throat,
These are the words poor Sidney cried,
'I hope you bloody well choke.'

Gwen Spriggs

Who?

The beckoning of war bids
I feel sorry for the women and kids
Who is the eye behind the rifle sight?
Who presses the button to put missiles into flight?
Who burdens the guilt for lives taken?
Who holds the consequences for misery making?
Who has that right and power
To make he nameless cower?
Who will be the victims to die?
Who will be the families to be mourned
As another day of war is dawned?
Who will mend the injured and the sick?
Who will take the lives they pick?
Who will mend broken memories left behind?
Who will give sight for those who are blind?
Lands and buildings we can replace
But not those lost, behind a name and face.

Terry J Powell

Collision Course

I blow you a kiss in the night,
Hoping it won't be intercepted in mid-flight.
But should it collide with one coming from you
The impact of our love must surely be true.

Heather Williamson

Tempered By The Weather

We British are honed and tempered by the constant rain
Leaden skies which greet us each day yet again
Stoical and ready to cope with each new downpour
Facing the elements with an outlook that is dour
Discussing the weather is the national occupation
Anxiously gazing up at the skies with trepidation
But anyone who can cope with the British weather
Develops a strong character that is as tough as leather
Setbacks and problems, both, we take them in our stride
Calmly taking them on shoulders so tough and wide
But last summer, shock of shocks, was dry and hot
Day after day we rose to find sunshine was our lot
We grumbled that it was too hot to do our work
Many of the demanding jobs we had to shirk
We sought the beaches and the swimming pools
As one by one we, guiltily at first, downed our tools
If instead of rainy days we have hot summers instead
Why, our national character will be turned on its head
We will be a lazy, slow and indolent race
Being constantly warmed by the sun on one's face.

Margaret Meagher

Born Again?

I woke up this morning
With a cold in the head
I'm surprised I woke up
Cos I thought I was dead!

Betty Nevell

MOMMY PLEASE

I'm filled with fear, always have been way of life,
Death was foremost in my mind,
Even by the age of five.

Born into a family,
Full of negativity, no room for light,
Started washing hands, at first just twice,
Progressed to three goes on,
Still the black, no room for light.

Superstition haunted me, always had to count to three,
Mustn't step on pavement lines,
Shoes on table, bad luck all day,
Don't walk under ladders, no other way.

Managed to survive to adulthood,
Children came, should never have been.
My obsession turned to them,
Couldn't go out in case they died, oh Mommy please they cried.

Stomach tight, panic there, nothing changed, fears still there,
Going out now, won't be long,
Must check the gas taps,
I know they're not on.

Carol Brierley

In Memory Of My Dearest Nan

Elizebeth Margeret Thompson was my nan, I am so proud to say,
And I loved her so much in every way,
I loved the way she looked after her hair,
And mismatched her lipstick and nails, she wouldn't dare.

Most people called her Betty as she was better known,
And I can honestly say you never heard her moan,
She would often sit me down and talk about the years that had passed,
And couldn't believe how they had flown by so fast.

She would often comment on the Yanks in their smart army suits,
Their straight, starched shirts and black shiny boots,
A little smile of happiness would appear on my nan's dear face,
As she looked back and remembered that time and happy place.

She would often baby-sit most weekends,
I'm sure Lucy and I used to drive her around the bend,
We also got a taste of my nan's famous choc chip cakes,
As did all her neighbours and friends, they used to know
she loved to bake.

Generous, thoughtful, kind - these were just some of the qualities
of my nan,
And I can truly say I was her number one fan,
Not only was she a nan, she was my best friend too,
Now you've gone I don't know what I'm going to do.

I'm going to miss you so very much,
Your little smile and gentle touch,
I know you will always be there for me by my side,
To look after me as I take every stride.

All your memories are in my heart to keep,
And that's a treasured place they will be buried down so deep,
As you Nan was the best,
So I'm going to say goodbye now and lay you to rest.

You will be forever in my heart,
Love Leigh.

Sharon Campbell Jay

A FENLAND RIVER

During the winter it's dark and unforgiving,
Heavy clouds gather as the mist is descending,
Gangs of seagulls can be seen swooping and diving
Searching for food to keep them from dying.
For them it's not hostile, it's a safe sanctuary,
From the storms and the turbulence they would face out at sea.
It's a permanent home for both mallard and teal,
It provides food for them all to have a square meal!

On a warm summer day it's a sight to behold,
As the sunlight transforms it to diamonds and gold,
Visitors languish on its banks of lush green,
Whilst a family of swans give their feathers a preen.
Fishermen wait patiently for that tug on their float,
Silently cursing a chugging narrow-boat.
Long, balmy days give way to warm, humid nights,
Owls slowly waking to begin their night flights.

The landscape vivid red as the sun sinks on the horizon,
Sunset in the fens - a spectacle you can rely on,
Reflections of warm colours embracing the water so still,
Surrounded by such beauty - who needs a hill?

Margaret Howlett

DEATH'S RATTLE

Lapis eyes sparkle, so lightly
Her skin becoming lifeless, so pale
A smile touches her lips, so slightly
Her trapped soul escaping its jail
The sun plays on her hair, so soft
Her breathing is slowing, so faint
Her throat becomes dry, she coughed
Her eyelids flutter, so quaint
Crimson blood at her lips, so sly
Making a sound, softer than a moan
Tears drip, she begins to cry
Tears of blood, so alone
The stars drip down as heat
Her life is ink on page
One last sigh, so sweet
A forest bird escaping its cage
She sees the opening door
Life's last and final battle
Her soul's chains drop to the floor
Come closer, you'll hear Death's rattle

Becky Keeling (14)

ANIMAL KINGDOM

Will toads still jump?
Will dogs still bark?
Will there still be one singing lark?

Will there still be fish swimming around
From dawn to sundown?

Will birds still fly?
Will hedgehogs still pass by?

Will mice still squeak?
Will squirrels still scamper?
Will there still be a furry hamster?

Will leopards still give a fright?
Will sharks still give a nasty bite?

Will ostriches still run fast?
Will cows still graze in a field of grass?

Will turtles still give birth?
Will moles still dig in the earth?

Will these animals still be about,
Or will all of these have died out?

Callum Stewart (9)

The Beautiful Garden

When I sleep at night-time
I have so many dreams,
I dream about my ideal garden
With lots of flowers and trees.

I think about the wind
Whistling through my hair,
I wish my garden was open and public
For the world to share.

I watch the flowers blossom,
The seeds turn into trees,
With lots of little honey pots
And many busy bees.

Look at the seasons changing,
The months going round and round,
I really have the ideal garden
Of which I am so proud.

So when I wake up
And my garden is no more,
I'll describe my garden to my friends
And tell them what I saw.

Adam Hedge (10)

CAN DOGGY POO BE BANNED?

As I wander round the town
With a poo bag in my hand,
I hope the day will come
When dog poo can be banned.
I think there should be rules and regs
That gives each dog the goal
Of learning how to cross their legs
And practice self-control.
Then at some pre-selected time,
(Say for instance half past nine,)
Every dog must quickly find
Some convenient roadside drain,
Quietly sit and wait for rain.
Then when the rain begins to fall,
Each dog may answer nature's call.
But some dogs will not meekly sit,
Some will do their doggy bit
Not in the rain or down the drain,
But just where we will step in it!
And thus ensuring every shoe
Carries its share of doggy poo.
The question spreads throughout the land,
Can doggy poo be really banned?

Richard Langridge

Out Of The Blue

Just a girl without a clue
Knows everything yet nothing
Black and blue
Into another door she will walk
He knows she will never talk
Softly, gently apologies flow
Deep down he knows she will not go
He slithers down the path, key in the door
Her heart rate increases, more to endure
Everyday she intends to leave, why does she opt to believe
For change he does not
She knows he won't stop
Piece by piece he takes her apart
Her mind, her body and then her heart
Where's the girl gone from so long ago, that smile she did
                                                            no longer know
Out of her prison a rainbow of flowers, a world to belong
She knows it's time to be strong
For he is insane
She's not to blame
She walks down life's path
Knowing not to look back
Black and blue she will no longer be
I know this because she was me.

Tina Brailey

It's Raining

Sitting on the window sill, holding the tears back
The stars have disappeared from the sky; there is just black
People walking around all with somewhere to go
What I'm doing with my life I just don't seem to know
Can't figure out what's going on
But at the moment it definitely feels wrong
I'm drifting away, everything is confusion
Can't talk to him, think I'm going to lose him
He's changed lately, not the person I knew
I want to talk to him, but just don't know how to
Way up high everything looks so small
But I know I'm setting myself up for a fall
I need to make a decision somehow
Everything these days ends up in a row
If I wasn't here, it wouldn't need to be done
They could carry on with their lives, would see the sun
Problems wouldn't exist for me up there
Well I don't know what happens when you're dead to be fair
Maybe I would feel nothing, or maybe pain
No matter what though, it would stop the rain
I wish I could just get it over with
If it were up to me I would no longer live

Charlotte Watkins

TINKY'S GONE

He looked at us with downcast eyes
So weak and tired was he.
We watched him with a heavy heart
His pain we did not see.

Then one day he fell about
On his legs he could not stand.
Time had come without a doubt
For us - to lend a hand.

We wrapped him gently in a towel
And took him to the vet.
Conscious of a deed most foul
And a dignity we won't forget.

Purring loudly he closed his eyes
We've helped him on his way.
Tinky's gone now, and we've said goodbye
It's in the garden forever our old cat will stay.

Sheila Podesta

ALL WILL BE WELL

Golden western sky
With rays like Heaven's pathways
Leading us to God
In His home beyond those clouds.
All is well. All will be well.

Doreen Lawrence

The Now

Beyond the world of ifs, buts and maybes
Away from the pressure of dreams
Hand in hand with me the now is present
Yesterday and tomorrow left on the bench.
There is no unseen threat
And no plans to get
Only the sun on my back
Encouraging the slack
Peace,
No race,
Or haste
For while the now is here
There is no hurt to fear.

Pete Harris

Old Photos

Old photos, like old friends, stay true
no matter how or what we do.
They show things just the way they were
in faded tints of sepia.

The grave young man in coat and tie,
who stands so stiff as time ticks by,
still rests his hand upon the chair,
of the stern faced lady sitting there.

Another photo clearly shows
the couple in a later pose.
But, time goes by. Now I am here,
as are the photos - and the chair!

Ztan Zmith

Memories Of Our Holiday

We loaded up the motor home and started on our way,
Our destination was Wales which was about three hundred miles away.
We did not like the motorways, we felt the A roads are the best,
You can have a more leisurely drive and sometimes stop to rest.
Pulling into a lay-by beside a swift flowing stream,
We knew our holiday had started and was not just a dream.
Looking at the scenery with the mountains up so high,
Taking care not to hit the sheep walking aimlessly by.
When we were up high the houses looked like little dots,
When we were down in the valley, we found some beautiful spots.
Rivers flowing freely with lovely waterfalls by the score,
Peaceful, quiet nights sleeping while parked upon the moor.
Meeting lovely people, making friends and taking photographs,
Enjoying climbing up the mountains and having lots of laughs.
Too soon our holiday was over which caused us a little pain,
So we made a vow that some day soon we would return again.

Stan Gilbert

Unbeatable Sounds

Whispering sounds blown afar by a gentle breeze
Passionate echoes, abound in valley tease
Trickling streams, washing stone beds so white
Waiting to sparkle, with moonbeams so bright
Brings day close much nearer though daylight tries
To suppress the feather folks' cries encircle the skies
Now dark clouds appearing blanket the scene
As silence, once more quiets the unbeatable sounds back to
                                                tranquillity serene

B Wharmby

I Think Of You

I think of you each day
So many, many times
I often wonder what to say
And how to give you signs

The way I want to feel and touch
The softness of your skin
I want to love you very much
This cannot be a sin.

Your lips beckon me to kiss you
It's so difficult to resist you
The soft curve of your mouth
The warm touch of your breath.

I long to hear those words
I know you wish to say
Give me your love and take me
Please take me away.

I would like to grant your wishes
And make your dreams come true
This will never be a crisis
It's the best for me and you.

You have already told me
How much you understand
Now can you really show me
You will always be my friend.

John L Pierrepont

THE KNIGHTS

Brave men, in fact and fable
Sitting round King Arthur's table
All of this valiant company
Wearing the order of chivalry
For courage and abilities
In time of hostilities
Strange stories we were told
Of these supermen of old
These knights were held in awe
For virtue in peace and war
From crusades in desert and wilderness
To rescuing damsels in distress
In armour bright on their steeds
Riding forth where honour leads
But times are not like they were
Another way of becoming Sir
Is to make sure you are seen
Exhibiting yourself on stage and screen
You don't need a lance and squire
A microphone you will require
Some say knighthoods can be bought
Or if you're a favourite at court
Perhaps you might be the sort
That gets a living out of sport
Many, I forgot their names
Are titled now for playing games
Nowadays it's not the bolder
Who gets a sword tap on the shoulder

Vic Calladine

THE HAUNTED HOUSE

There it was again
Footsteps on the stairs
She opened the bedroom door
But couldn't see what was in front of her face
Downstairs she could smell burning
Nothing had been cooked
It only lasted seconds then the smell was gone
To bed she went, the room was very cold
She could hear whispering, she looked but she was all alone
She stood in front of her mirror brushing her wavy hair
She could hear heavy breathing next to her ear
Panic set in her heart, fright took over her
For now her heart was racing but she was still alert
From that moment on she knew what she must do
The old lady came with a cross and some salt
Every room was blessed by her
She prayed for the departed souls
To move on into the light
She prayed they would never return
And hoped at last
They had found their place
And not Earth bound to this home

Sharon Lambley Dzus

BEDTIME BABY

It's way past his bedtime
I wish it was mine
But he simply will not go
Just hope that his daddy doesn't know

Will he keep still?
Now he's saying there is a chill
Go to sleep just give me a hug
Just my dressing gown gets a tug

It's way past his bedtime
If his daddy comes will he be fine?
I kiss his little head
And gently carry him to bed

Will he keep still?
Wow this bedtime lark is such a skill
I smile and turn
Will I ever learn?

Come on then 5 minutes more
And head towards the door
A patter of little feet
And he's on the chair all curled up neat

His eyes he does close
And rubs his tiny nose
At last he's drifting
And again I lift him

My baby goodnight
I hold you so tight
God keep you safe and warm
And for evermore

Sarah Tyrrell

DEPRESSION (THE ACCUSED)

We pass the tear sent laughter
And idle with the thoughtless mind
With the essence of a love once given
In the song which once was mine

Abide by the rule be you joker or fool
Cast aside the day you spoke
Walk away and don't come back I say
For the wheel of fortune is broke

Like a fine wine that matures with age
Is the hate that grows like cancer
Eating away at the truths of the day
Never letting you near the answer

Soaked are the feet which passed the door
Soaked in the dirt of the lie
The one which was told by the young to the old
The one which will never die

The jury sit impatient and sigh
The accused stands straight and rigid
Harmed is the one sitting weak and blind
Growing more weak and more frigid

Sentence was passed in the week called nine
Black hat was placed on head
The accused did cry, *'What was my life?'*
The harmed could not cry, she was dead

Rachel Kate

INSPIRATIONAL

Inspirational where madam,
Writes her memoirs and letters,
Whilst listening to sublime music,
Of yesteryears' musicians.

Serene, graceful and inspirational,
Oh come darling softer than a blossoming rose,
Underneath those colossal, powerful stars,
Reading nothing but muse.

With piano in full revolt,
With moonlight sonata fading,
Within your mind and heart,
With temperament of a king.

Will-O-The-Wisp, alluring,
Singing compensating your charms,
Indefatigable and consuming,
Where moon lilies grow in abundance.

To that inspirational dance,
Longing, longing for love,
When romancing giving your heart away,
Where the danseur brings astonishment and joy.

Oh heavenly purpose,
With overtures of beauty strong,
Within the garden landscape,
Is but simple paradise musing.

With the simplicity of love,
Locked within your treasured heart,
Where came down a singing dove,
From miles up above.

With magical embrace,
On a secret note of grace,
Love champions spiritually,
As I look dearly upon your face.

To the overture of classical taste,
The sublime music plays beautifully,
To all those who appreciate,
A triumphant sound of beauties' melody.

With blessings of a blessed love,
Inside the interior of one's heart.

James S Cameron

TRANQUILLITY

As the ocean waters pass you by,
The tranquillity's enough to make you cry,
Not with sadness, but joy by far,
Our Heavenly Earth is what you are.

The blue of the sky on a sunny day,
The cotton wool clouds that pass away,
Warmth from the sun upon your face,
Eyes close, the memories begin to chase.

The beauty of a budding flower,
A tree that grows hour by hour,
Birds and bees fly by with no care,
Each day brings us, a new breath of air.

A colourful rainbow along with the gold,
A mind that's so wonderful, be it new or old,
The twinkling stars, that watch over us,
Along with our Lord without any fuss.

Jacqueline Ann

TOGETHERNESS

Peter and I have a captive audience
so our thoughts we can release
You all chose to be here
and give our minds peace

This room is full of so much love
it's bursting at the seams
Giving us the confidence
to realise our dreams

Touching our lives from time to time
knowing you'll all be there
Being here today shows
just how much you all care

Now we are one travelling
the path of life
Sharing our feelings
our troubles and strife
We'll need your help
to see us through
Be there for us
as we will for you

Friends come here to be with us
on our special day
The unity between us all
must never fade away.

Joan Marrion

THE NIGHT SKY

The sands are blown,
The wind does whistle,
I am alone.
The clear, crystal night sky
Looks down upon me,
Alone in the sands.
The sky's compassionate eyes
Mirror the loneliness,
The emptiness.

A wind blows the dunes,
They ripple like water,
With the movement of a rattlesnake.
I stand, here in the desert,
In the sands,
The emptiness.

Time seems frozen
As I wander through the desert,
Sand grains tickle my feet,
As a cool calmness surrounds me.
I spot an oasis, magical and twinkling,
Under the stars.

The water seems solid,
But the slightest ripple gives it away,
A mirror,
A gem,
A magical drop from a star,
Here in the desert
Under the twinkling night's eye,
Just me, the sky and sand.

Emily Lunn (12)

Our Baby, Our Boss!
1990-2003
Little Daisy Dolittle Devlin

Through your life you were a star shining bright,
The angels will recognise your special little light.
You were a precious spirit, we will miss you so much,
You brought such happiness to all the lives you touched.

Children adored you, greeted you with glee,
We will never forget you, your dad, Duds and me.

You're in doggy heaven now, and we know for a fact,
That the weather is perfect, you'll really like that.
Every day a Daisy Day, a warm and gentle breeze,
And you'll be met by old, dear friends,
Like Oliver, Jellybean and of course, Lovely Lucy.

You loved to swim and rub your face in the snow,
If your legs had been longer, you'd have loved it even more!

Your dad was your hero, You were his special treasure,
And Duds, your devoted husband, loved you beyond measure.

Your babies were beautiful, you were such a great mummy,
But then, you were always very proud of your tummy.

Photographs by the score, strangers knocking at the door,
All wanted to know you, have you as their friend.
And now this unique little spirit,
To the angels we send.

Your portrait had been painted, even books been written,
We're quite sure even the Archangel will be smitten.
We're told there's a magical place just this side of a rainbow,
Where puppies like you receive their wings and halos.

You travelled the world, always in style,
Your elegant bag made everyone smile.
Your hero carried you everywhere as the years passed by,
There were a hundred reasons you were the apple of his eye.

You've been carried to Heaven on cardinal's wings,
But who will wake us for breakfast before the birds sing?
Who will be our confidant and listen to our troubles,
And do a little dance for her dinner, and reward us with cuddles?
Who will demand to be carried to the top of the stair,
And fall asleep snoring on top of our hair?

You kept us all together, together through thick and thin,
Your life had such great meaning, no heart you couldn't win.
Until the last you were a puppy, never seeming old,
Always affectionate, entertaining, cheeky and very, very bold.
We will hold your memory in our hearts,
Carry you along our way.
And when we all come together again,
It will be the most glorious Daisy Day.

Your devoted mum, dad & Duds

Gillian Corrigan Devlin

TIME IS TICKING

I'm tumbling, I'm falling
The past chases me and touches me
I won't look back, but I must
Deeper and deeper into life
On and on it moves
For heaven's sake, slow down!
I haven't been anywhere yet
I haven't done anything yet
Now you are trying to rush me
Let go of me and give me freedom
I'll get up an hour early, every day
That's it, more time available
Deeper and deeper out of dark
I'm tumbling, I'm falling
Life just keeps calling
Love, lust and taste
It's all there you know
In the shop window of life!
I keep looking around its shelves
But can't decide what to purchase
Anything for my half a century?
The other half is calling.

John Carter

MY DADDY
(For Emily)

When you were a little child did you ever feel pushed out
The one who lacked the sympathy and who received the shout?
I remember my sister, so much older than I
When Dad came home from working he would lift her very high
And plant a kiss upon her cheek while I waited close behind
He never seemed to cuddle me or have me on his mind
I never sat upon his knee or felt his loving arms
I just received his angry voice and the hardness of his palms
I could never understand just what I had done wrong
For Daddy not to hold me in his arms for which I longed
Other people cuddled me when to the house they came
But it wasn't like my daddy's touch I needed, but in vain
I know that I was awkward and always falling down
But I tried so hard to do what's right and still he looked and frowned
I loved my sister dearly and would give her all I had
If only I could share the love that she had with my dad

Grace Divine

BEING THE SOFA FOR DOCTOR WHO

The decade I did miss,
Not setting aside time.
How I've missed Doctor Who and the Tardis,
Wondering if Sarah Jane Smith still owns K9.
This I will never know.

Only its return has a reputation to master,
Looking behind the sofa at BBC One.
Viewing figures have a lot to answer,
That persuaded the Daleks and Cybermen that they've won.
Before the cliff-hanger preferred the credits to show.

Alex Billington

THE SEA

Winter tides roaring with anger
heaving shingle high upon the beach,
waves sucked back gaining momentum,
before bowling as far as they can reach.

Released from the summer straightjacket,
now determined to have its fling,
making up for lost time in confinement,
the sea truly calls the tune to sing.

A warning to all those seafarers,
who think they can master the sea,
the hand that controls the tempest,
was the hand that created you and me.

J H Bennetts

HOPE LOST

A man sits alone by the fire and weeps
He has tried several times, but just cannot sleep
His wife and two bairns are tucked up tight
They won't awake until after daylight
With nothing to eat, no money to buy
He stares at the embers, and sometimes the sky
The sky is like velvet, seems studded with stars
That twinkle like diamonds held up in glass jars
The pits are all gone - work prospects are poor
The man sits and thinks on the sitting room floor
He stands and goes out to the comforting sky
Takes rope from the shed, making his choice to die.

Jayne Shepherd

FOUR LETTER WORDS!

Trim poem, only just!
Four word line - must.
Five, won't make fame,
Nine, fail - same game.

More seem like lust,
Turn some into dust.
Keep them well away;
'Curt', 'tiny' - hold sway.

'Find task most hard',
Thus said poet Bard.
Then came mind lift,
Mist gone - find gift.

Skip fast over page,
Soon done, gone rage.
Easy flow, last line
This will suit fine.

Gerald S Bell

GUILT

I was walking in the meadows,
On a lovely summer's day,
The sky was blue,
The grass was high,
And flowers in array.
I picked a bunch of buttercups,
All yellow and aglow,
But before they got to water,
Their heads were drooping so.

Jacqueline Ann Johnston

Harry Who?

The Harry that I loved was straight and tall,
Rather austere, yet kindly too.
He rode his horse to battle in the First World War.

Stayed around to help restore,
Then stayed to reach for 2 years more.

On his return no job there was for him,
For this hero there was no cheer.
Save ongoing welcome from all his kith and kin,
Who wanted all the best for him.

For indeed
He was a hero,
My uncle.

Dolly Harmer

Sunday Tea

I remember how it used to be,
When great Aunt Leasha came to tea,
Always with chocolates and trifle she came,
Up on the bus from old Awsworth Lane.
We'd all sit down to a wonderful spread,
Tinned salmon and ham and freshly baked bread.
Then out came the cards, a penny a game,
Though most of the winnings Aunt Leasha would claim.
Then just before eight she'd walk to the stop,
The one across from the old corner shop,
Home to Park Hill down old Awsworth Lane,
Since then Sunday teas were never the same.

Mark L Moulds

OVER A RAINBOW

The wind was slow
The sky was blue
Over a rainbow
I met you.

I saw your face
And immediately knew
That nothing would be better
Than becoming friends with you.

I watched you move
I saw you say
Something like
'What a beautiful day.'

You said, 'Hello'
And shook my hand
Then I secretly knew
I was glad with what I'd found!

Shaheen Akhtar (15)

Untitled

To *never* want her to leave my side
To *never* want to sleep
To *never* want to let go of her hand
To *never* want her to drift out of sight

To *always* want to smell her skin
To *always* want to feel her presence
To *always* want to hear her laugh
To *always* want to see her smile

To *sometimes* want to lay and cuddle
To *sometimes* want to walk for miles
To *sometimes* want to stand and stare
To *sometimes* want to never let go

Never alone
Always together
Sometimes it feels like I've known her forever

This, to me, is how love should be.

Joanne Patchett

DAILY REFLECTIONS ON BEING A MUM

Being a mum is not all it's cracked up to be,
Having a child is painful as can be,
24 hours a day at a baby's beck and call,
Days when crying drives you up the wall.

Hard to share your home with a little someone new,
You try to welcome them and keep them warm too,
Here comes the baby with a lot of stress,
Housework not done and the house is a mess.

Washing today and tomorrow too,
No 'free time' for poor old you,
Make a bottle and give a feed,
No time to sit or to read.

When I look back across them years,
Three children grown-up,
1 daughter and 2 sons,
And now my daughter she's a mum.

Today I reflect on my eldest son,
He was number 1,
He has died and I have cried and cried,
A burden less and I have distress.

My youngest boy,
My pride and joy,
Achieves such a lot, he's determined and strong,
As this always helps to make him a good son,
To me his dear old mum.

God bless each and everyone!

Jo Willbye

IT SEEMS LIKE ONLY YESTERDAY

Gone is the face so dear, also her eyes so clear
Gone is the skin so fair, also her silken hair
Gone is the waist so trim, also her legs so slim

Gone like footprints in the sand,
when the tide comes in.

Worn eyes with crow's feet now, grey hair and wrinkled brow
Rotund tum, ample seat, widened girth, swollen feet
Unseen by husband dear, only the love so clear

A noble, gallant smile
Reflects his stalwart heart

Gone is the strong young man, also his rugged tan
Gone is the thick, dark hair, also his shoulders square
Gone is the firm young chin, also his waist so slim

Gone like snowflakes on the trees,
when the thaw sets in

Faded eyes, bloodshot now, bald head with furrowed brow
Bent back with puckered butt, weak chest, extended gut
Unseen by wife so true, only her love still new

A genteel winsome smile
Reflects her loving heart

Winsome Mary Payter

TIME TO GO

Remember when the chips were down
Left lying in the fire?
Where the ceiling was like the feeling
It couldn't get much higher
And that Cornish violin
That played a plaintive tune
Ev'ry the day the sun came up
It's now eclipsed by gloom
Our castle lies in ruins
But the steaks still fry
For a final encounter
When the stakes were high
Try to shed my nightmares
Leave them in the hall
But the ghost of derision
Still can't wait to call
Now our train is off the rails
It ain't goin' home
Go and live your tortured life
And leave me alone
How do you function?
Go down the entry . . .
Or up the junction?
It's like a scenic railway
That's run out of track
It's just a roller coaster
That ain't coming back

Graham Punter

INFORMATION

We hope you have enjoyed reading this book - and that you will continue to enjoy it in the coming years.

If you like reading and writing poetry drop us a line, or give us a call, and we'll send you a free information pack.

Alternatively if you would like to order further copies of this book or any of our other titles, then please give us a call or log onto our website at www.forwardpress.co.uk

**Anchor Books Information
Remus House
Coltsfoot Drive
Peterborough
PE2 9JX
(01733) 898102**